Sukhoi S-37 and Mikoyan MFI

Russian Fifth-Generation Fighter Technology Demonstrators

Yefim Gordon

Original translation by Dmitriy Komissarov

Midland Publishing

**Mikoyan MFI and Sukhoi S-37
Russian Fifth-Generation Fighter Technology
Demonstrators**
© 2001 Yefim Gordon
ISBN 1 85780 120 2

Published by Midland Publishing
4 Watling Drive, Hinckley
LE10 3EY, England
Tel: 01455 254 490   Fax: 01455 254 495
E-mail: midlandbooks@compuserve.com

Midland Publishing is an imprint of
Ian Allan Publishing Ltd

All rights reserved. No part of this
publication may be reproduced,
stored in a retrieval system, transmitted
in any form or by any means, electronic,
mechanical or photo-copied, recorded
or otherwise, without the written
permission of the publishers.
Quotations from this publication shall
contain a reference to the source.

Worldwide distribution (except North America):
Midland Counties Publications
4 Watling Drive, Hinckley
LE10 3EY, England
Telephone: 01455 233 747   Fax: 01455 233 737
E-mail: midlandbooks@compuserve.com

North American trade distribution:
Specialty Press Publishers & Wholesalers Inc.
11605 Kost Dam Road, North Branch, MN 55056
Tel: 651 583 3239   Fax: 651 583 2023
Toll free telephone: 800 895 4585

Design concept and layout by
Polygon Press Ltd
Colour artwork by Valentin Vetlitskiy

Printed in England by
Ian Allan Printing Ltd
Riverdene Business Park, Molesey Road,
Hersham, Surrey, KT12 4RG

This book has been jointly prepared
with Polygon Press Ltd, Moscow

The Sukhoi S-37 Berkoot fighter technology demonstrator completes its landing run in Zhukovskiy.

Contents

The Concept is Born 5
Multi-mission MiG 11
S-37: Proud Bird of Prey 49
'To be or not to be?' 81

In writing this book the author has made use of unclassified information published in various sources. These include the newspapers Nezavisimoye voyennoye obozreniye (Independent Military Review, a weekly supplement to the Nezavisimaya gazeta/ Independent Newspaper daily) and Krasnaya zvezda (Red Star, the Russian Ministry of Defence daily); the magazines Ves'nik aviatsii i kosmonavtiki/ Aerospace Herald, Aviatsiya – Kosmonavtika (Aviation and Spacefaring), Tekhnika i vo'oroozheniye (Equipment and Weaponry), Air Fleet, Flight International, Aviation Week & Space Technology, Air International, Air & Cosmos, Jane's Defence Weekly etc; the book 60 Years of the Mikoyan OKB, as well as press releases of Russian aerospace companies and recordings of press conferences held at various international airshows.

This book is illustrated by photos by Yefim I. Gordon, Viktor G. Drooshlyakov, Aleksey V. Mikheyev, the Sukhoi OKB and RSK MiG (MiG Russian Aircraft Company).

'We are sure that many of the ideas incorporated in the *izdeliye* 1.44' development aircraft can be used for developing a fifth-generation fighter. We have a fairly clear idea of how Russia's fifth-generation fighter should look. Moreover, we are now working on a long-range plan taking into account the economic and political situation of today. The test results [obtained with the 1.44] shall form a stable basis for RSK MiG's next-generation fighter proposals for the Russian Air Force and Air Defence Force.'

Nikolay F. NIKITIN
General Director and General Designer, RSK MiG

'AVPK Sukhoi are investigating and verifying advanced technologies on the S-37 Berkoot forward-swept wing development aircraft. These will become features of Russia's next-generation fighter.

...The implementation of the new-generation fighter programme is of crucial importance for developing Russia's aircraft industry and strengthening its positions on the world market. Unless we solve this task, the aircraft industry has no future.'

Mikhail A. POGOSYAN
General Director, AVPK Sukhoi

The Concept is Born

Mikoyan MFI and Sukhoi S-37

Above: The Dassault Rafale is the best French fourth-generation fighter incorporating the latest airframe and avionics technologies. Illustrated is the Rafale C01, the first production aircraft for the *Armée de l'Air*.

Below: A Lockheed Martin (General Dynamics) F-16A Fighting Falcon tactical fighter.

The military doctrine generally accepted in the final decades of the 20th century included the possibility of wars waged with conventional (non-nuclear) weapons. Analysis of past armed conflicts and potential war scenarios showed that neither side could win the war without gaining air superiority – and state-of-the-art fighters were the key weapons system, the key element in reaching this goal.

The USA was the first nation to start development of fourth-generation fighters; the first of these were the McDonnell Douglas (now Boeing) F-15 Eagle and the General Dynamics (now Lockheed Martin) F-16 Fighting Falcon. The Soviet Union countered by developing the Mikoyan MiG-29 *Fulcrum* and Sukhoi Su-27 *Flanker* which were markedly superior to their American counterparts as regards combat potential. This is especially true for the MiG-29 versus F-16, since the initial F-16A had neither medium-range air-to-air missiles (AAMs) nor infra-red search & track (IRST) unit, nor helmet-mounted sight (HMS).

The Americans got a head start once again when the US Air Force launched the ATF (Advanced Tactical Fighter) programme in 1981. A similar research and development effort was started in the USSR shortly afterwards as part of the R&D activities specified by the Soviet five-year economic development plans. Along with relatively conventional swept-wing designs, design teams in both nations contemplated more exotic layouts with forward-swept wings (FSW) offering better performance at transonic speeds.

The story of Mikoyan's and Sukhoi's next-generation fighters began in the mid-1970s when the Soviet aircraft industry and defence industry embarked on three large-scale R&D programmes called I-90 (*istrebitel'* – fighter), Sh-90 (*shtoormovik* – attack aircraft) and B-90 (*bombardeerovschchik* – bomber). The plan was to develop new-generation fighters, strike aircraft and strategic bombers that would enter service with the Soviet Air Force (VVS – *Voyenno-vozdooshnyye seely*) and the Air Defence Force (PVO – **Pro**tivo**voz**doosh**naya oborona**) in the 1990s.

This was a monstrous effort, and numerous institutions performed theoretical research and data analysis, trying to predict the trends in combat aircraft development. The I-90 fighter programme (the Soviet answer to

The Concept is Born

the ATF) involved at least five such establishments. The Ministry of Defence's TsNII-30 (*Tsentrahl'nyy naoochno-issledovatel'skiy institoot* – Central Research Institute) and NII-2 were tasked with drawing up general operational requirements for future tactical fighters and interceptors. The Central Aerodynamics & Hydrodynamics Institute named after Nikolay Ye. Zhukovskiy (TsAGI – *Tsentrahl'nyy aero- i ghidrodinamicheskiy institoot*) was to study alternative general arrangements, examining their strengths and weaknesses, and select the fighter's overall dimensions.

The Central Institute of Aero Engines (TsIAM – *Tsentrahl'nyy institoot aviatseeonnovo motorostroyeniya*) was to determine the parameters of advanced powerplants, air intake and nozzle types. Finally, the State Research Institute of Aircraft Systems (GosNII AS – *Gosoodahrstvennyy naoochno-issledovatel'skiy institoot aviatseeonnykh sistem*), one of the Soviet Union's leading avionics designers, would formulate the requirements for the fighter's weapons control system (including the radar), armament and survivability.

Actual work on the concept of Russia's fifth-generation fighter started in the early 1980s. The cornerstones of the concept were:

– ultra-manoeuvrability (this means the aircraft had to be capable of sustained flight at angles of attack (AoAs) of at least 60°);

– supercruise capability, ie, the ability to cruise at supersonic speed without using afterburner(s). The idea was that the afterburner(s) would be ignited only briefly to put on a burst of speed – eg, when intercepting an enemy aircraft or in order to gain a tactical advantage;

– stealth, ie, a low radar cross-section (RCS) and a low infra-red signature.

The aircraft had to incorporate new-generation weapons and a new avionics architecture with artificial intelligence. Markedly improving field performance and maintainability was also important. A fifth-generation fighter was to be capable of engaging multiple targets beyond visual range and have all-aspect engagement capability in a dogfight without making establishing visual contact with the target.

Developing a fifth-generation integrated avionics suite became one of the top priority areas. The avionics designers were facing the task of developing completely new data pre-

Above: A SAAB JAS-39B Gripen shows off its canard layout.

Below: A McDonnell Douglas F-15E Strike Eagle multi-role fighter from Edwards AFB. The F-15 is one of the best Western fourth-generation fighters.

Mikoyan MFI and Sukhoi S-37

Above: The Soviet Union developed two highly successful fourth-generation fighters. The Mikoyan MiG-29 *Fulcrum* was one of them; illustrated here is the first prototype of the upgraded MiG-29SMT (917 Blue).

Below: The other fourth-generation fighter which brought Soviet aircraft engineers worldwide fame was the Sukhoi Su-27. This is a stock example of the first production version, the *Flanker-B* (T10-S).

The Concept is Born

sentation modes. This applied to navigation tasks (displaying the aircraft's spatial orientation, co-ordinates and speed with regard to the terrain), as well as realistic presentation of objects on the ground and other aircraft.

'Situational awareness' was the key phrase as far as the avionics were concerned. The avionics suite was to:
– show threats on the ground and in the air, using three-dimensional visuals and sound;
– indicate the actions of friendly forces (so that the pilot can concentrate on priority threats, knowing that other targets are being taken care of by other aircraft);
– show weapons and electronic support measures (ESM) equipment status.

The Soviet fifth-generation fighter concept envisaged parallel development of two basic types. One was a twin-engined long-range heavy fighter with a powerful long-range radar and a large supply of missiles; the other was a single-engined light tactical fighter having the maximum possible degree of commonality with the 'heavy' type. Soviet researchers working on the concept made use of available information on the American ATF program.

According to Soviet tradition, development of advanced fighters under the I-90 programme proceeded on a competitive basis. The leading Soviet fighter design bureaux – OKB-155 named after Artyom Ivanovich Mikoyan, aka MMZ *Zenit* (Zenith), and OKB-51 named after Pavel Osipovich Sukhoi, aka MZ *Koolon* (Coulomb) – were ordered to submit their proposals. (OKB = **op**ytno-kon**strook**torskoye byuro – experimental design bureau (there were no 'companies' as such in the USSR); the number is a code allocated for security reasons. MMZ = *Moskovskiy ma**shin**ostroitel'nyy za**vod*** – Moscow Machinery Plant No. something-or-other; MMZ 'Zenit' or MMZ No. 155 was the name of Mikoyan's experimental shop.)

Interestingly, not all Soviet OKB heads were eager to take part in the programme. For instance, Yevgeniy A. Ivanov, who was then General Designer (the official title of Soviet/Russian design bureau heads*)* at Sukhoi, declined to participate, believing that the T-10 *Flanker-A* fourth-generation fighter then under development was the fighter of the 1990s. Ivanov was convinced that the potential of the T-10 (the predecessor of the production T10-S/ Su-27 *Flanker-B et seq.*) was such that this aircraft and its derivatives would not be surpassed by any other fighter designed before the end of the century. History showed that he was right.

Nevertheless, Minister of Aircraft Industry Ivan Silayev insisted that the Sukhoi OKB should participate in the I-90 programme and eventually got his way. Some time later Sukhoi submitted their proposal – a twin-engined fighter with forward-swept wings. This layout, which benefited from aerodynamic research performed by TsAGI and the Siberian Aviation Research Institute named after S. A. Chaplygin (SibNIA – *See**beer**skiy na**ooch**no-is**sled**ovatel'skiy insti**toot** avia**ht**sii*) in Novosibirsk, offered high agility, including good stability and control at AoAs of 90° or more.

The design bureau named after Aleksandr Sergeyevich Yakovlev, which is also known as OKB-115 or MMZ *Skorost'* (Speed), decided to join the race, too. Yakovlev had different views on fifth-generation fighter design, proposing a single-engined aircraft with a canard (tail-first) layout, delta wings and twin tails.

A Soviet fifth-generation fighter undergoing wind tunnel tests at SibNIA.

The Eurofighter EF2000 *Typhoon* has been ordered by several NATO nations; illustrated here is the second prototype, DA2, in Luftwaffe markings (98+29).

Mikoyan MFI and Sukhoi S-37

These four views illustrate the Yakovlev OKB's ill-starred attempt to create a fifth-generation fighter. Like the Mikoyan and Sukhoi competitors, it utilised the twin-tailed, canard arrangement. The single-engined layout killed the aircraft and it was never built. The photos show clearly that the fighter was to incorporate stealth features and thrust-vectoring control; note the unusual double-kinked wing and canard trailing edges.

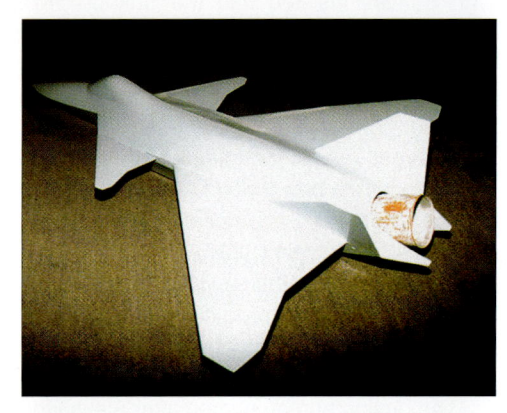

The photos below and right illustrate the sharply canted fins, the sharp nose chines and the lateral air intakes. The shape of the nose is remarkably similar to that of the Lockheed Martin F-22A Raptor.

The airframe incorporated a number of stealth features. Unusually, both wings and canard foreplanes had a double-kinked trailing edge. The vertical tails were strongly canted outwards. The forward fuselage with sharp chines was reminiscent of the Lockheed Martin F-22. The engine was to have a vectoring nozzle which moved only in the vertical plane.

However, the single-engined layout was the project's main weakness as far as the Soviet military were concerned. For the last twenty years the prevailing viewpoint among Russian military experts has been that a multi-role tactical aircraft shall have at least two engines – for better survivability if nothing else. Thus the Yakovlev fighter was rejected in favour of the multi-role tactical fighter developed by the Mikoyan OKB.

The Mikoyan contender also utilised the delta-wing, twin-tailed, canard layout. This arrangement offered certain advantages in supersonic cruise but could not match the FSW layout in manoeuvrability at transonic speeds.

The Air Force's selection of Mikoyan as the 'first choice' was politically motivated into the bargain. Quite simply, the Mikoyan OKB was then a highly specialised 'fighter maker'; diversification and development of aircraft in other categories did not come until much later. The rival Sukhoi OKB, on the other hand, worked in a much wider area, designing fighters, attack aircraft and tactical bombers. One can hardly blame the Soviet military for wanting to support Mikoyan, since the Sukhoi OKB was less dependent on whether it would get the new-generation fighter 'contract' or not. Finally, while Sukhoi were breaking new ground with their FSW project, the Mikoyan fighter was built along more conventional lines and represented a lower technical risk.

Multi-mission MiG

Mikoyan MFI and Sukhoi S-37

Taking shape

As mentioned earlier, in the early 1980s, some time before the VVS chose the 'main contractor' for their fifth-generation fighter, the Mikoyan OKB and other Soviet fighter design bureaux were tasked with developing a fighter that would counter the threat posed by the as-yet unbuilt American ATF. Mikoyan engineers worked on two parallel projects – a twin-engined heavy multi-role tactical fighter provisionally designated MFI (**mno**gofoonktsio**nahl**'nyy fronto**voy** istre**bitel**') and a single-engined light tactical fighter, or LFI (**lyoh**kiy fronto**voy** istre**bitel**'). The MFI bore the manufacturer's designation 'project 512' (at a later stage of the work it was commonly referred to as 'iz**deli**ye 5.12'), while the LFI was known in-house as 'project 412' or 'izdeliye 4.12'). (Izdeliye (product) such and such is a code commonly used for military hardware items.)

(**Note:** The author of one feature on the MFI published in the Russian press suggested that the product code 'izdeliye 5.12' was chosen with a view to fooling Western intelligence agencies into thinking this was yet another version of the well-known MiG-29 if any information leaked out by accident. Cf. MiG-29/izdeliye 9.12 Fulcrum-A, MiG-29/izdeliye 9.13 Fulcrum-C, MiG-29S/izdeliye 9.13S Fulcrum-C, MiG-29UB/izdeliye 9.51 Fulcrum-B and so on. However, this does not appear credible for two reasons. Firstly, the manufacturer's designations of all MiG-29 versions begin with a 9, not with a 5; secondly, experience shows that these izdeliye designations were usually allocated at random.)

The MFI and LFI were to share as many components as possible. Additionally, the bigger MFI was to have several specialised versions (no further details are available as to what versions were considered).

Most R&D establishments in the defence, aerospace and electronics industries had more work than they could handle. Also, development of the fifth-generation fighter and its systems and equipment was a complex affair, and development costs and the complexity of the work grew higher and higher. All this led the Soviet government to formulate a so-called Combined Task Programme in 1983 with the purpose of developing new systems and technologies to be used in all classes of aircraft. The programme was also meant to improve the interaction of various institutions and ministries, reducing bureaucratic red tape and maximising efficiency.

V. N. Schchepin, the Mikoyan OKB's preliminary design (PD) section chief, was one of the 'fathers' of the Combined Task Programme. Mikoyan General Designer Rostislav Apollosovich Belyakov supported the idea. Presently the programme was approved by the VVS and industry 'top brass'; the Mikoyan OKB became the primary 'contractor' to develop the MFI and LFI, and the programme was included into the five-year economic development plan. In 1983 the VVS, the PVO and the Ministry of Aircraft Industry (MAP – Mi**nister**stvo aviatsee**on**noy pro**mysh**lennosti) jointly tasked the OKB with drawing up provisional specifications of its fifth-generation fighter.

PD studies of the MFI (project 512) and LFI (project 412) ran for several years. As noted earlier, numerous research establishments, including TsAGI, were actively involved in formulating the concept. After a lot of theoretical studies and wind tunnel research TsAGI engineers recommended that Mikoyan should use the canard layout for the MFI, since it gave the required agility and offered maximum lift for a statically unstable aircraft with an aft CG position. The aircraft was to have large delta wings with a leading-edge sweep of 40 to 45°, an internal weapons bay or at least provisions for conformal (semi-recessed) weapons carriage. The variable air intake was to be located ventrally for maximum efficiency during sharp manoeuvres (especially high-alpha manoeuvres) and throughout the speed range, including supersonic speeds. The fighter was to feature thrust-vectoring control (TVC) providing ultra-manoeuvrability and short take-off and landing (STOL) capability.

Preliminary development of the MFI involved an unparalleled number of wind tunnel hours and unprecedented scale model tests aimed at measuring the aircraft's RCS, verifying air intake and engine nozzle perfor-

A wind tunnel model of an early configuration of *izdeliye* 1.42.

Another early wind tunnel model used to determine the air intake design. This view shows well the common V-shaped intake with central splitter which was planned for the production MFI (1.42).

mance. A common intake for both engines and two-dimensional (rectangular) vectoring nozzles were evaluated, among other configurations. Flight control actuators, radar components and avionics interfaces were tested. The optimum angle for the ejection seat was chosen and the possibility of altering this angle in flight (!) was contemplated in order to allow the pilot to pull higher-G manoeuvres. Side-stick controls and the possibility of using flexible cannons were studied, along with hundreds of other issues.

The design crystallised as the engineers worked with TsAGI wind tunnel test results, preliminary powerplant and avionics specifications, and the parameters of radar absorbent materials (RAM). The canard layout was approved and the fighters' dimensions were selected at this stage, along with the shape of the air intake, nozzles, vertical tails and ventral fins and the aircraft systems' principal parameters. In 1987 Mikoyan and the other organisations involved submitted the MFI and LFI PD projects for review – and got a thumbs-up.

Basically the projected fifth-generation MiGs differed from existing Soviet fighters in just about everything. First of all, they used the close-coupled canard layout and an adaptive wing design offering a high lift/drag ratio in both subsonic and supersonic mode, as well as the ability to fly at extreme AoAs and a high lift coefficient. The wings were cambered and featured leading-edge slats and flaperons.

Second, the fighters were to be powered by fifth-generation thrust-vectoring jet engines then under development at the Lyul'ka OKB (NPO Saturn, now Lyul'ka-Saturn). (NPO = na**ooch**no-proiz**vod**stvennoye obyedi**neni**ye – scientific and production association.) Besides having a high thrust/weight ratio, the engines were to be compact and easy to manufacture. Their specified thrust by far exceeded that of any engine used hitherto on tactical aircraft.

Third, the avionics had a hierarchical structure and artificial intelligence, utilising interactive controls. The flight instrumentation, weapons control system (WCS), electronic countermeasures (ECM), navigation and communications equipment were integrated into a single suite by multiplex databuses. Provisions were made for tactical information to be downloaded from or uploaded to ground command, control and communications (C³) centres via data link. Fourth, the avionics – as well as the weapons, which were also integrated into the aircraft's equipment suite – were to attain a new level of capability thanks to state-of-the-art electronic components.

Finally, the aircraft were to be operated and maintained on a 'technical condition' basis (rather than serviced at rigidly prescribed intervals, as was customary). As compared to existing designs they were to have a higher service life, lower maintenance requirements in terms of man-hours and reduced damage elimination time. This would be helped by using standardised line replaceable units (LRUs).

A new name

The PD projects of the LFI and MFI were taken further into the full-scale development stage. However, the Mikoyan OKB found it difficult to finance the development of two fifth-generation projects at once, so the LFI was shelved and engineers concentrated on the 'heavy' MFI. At this stage the aircraft received the designation under which it was to gain fame – *izdeliye* 1.42. Gheorgiy A. Sedov was appointed chief project engineer, with Yuriy P. Vorotnikov, A. S. Zazhigin and, a while later, V. M. Polyakov as his deputies (assistants). Vorotnikov was responsible for structural/systems design, Zazhigin for financing and prototype manufacturing, and Polyakov for the avionics suite. (The usual practice at Soviet OKBs was that the chief project engineer was tasked with overall project co-ordination while his deputies were responsible for various aspects of the actual design process.) Since the MFI project was a high-priority one, General Designer Rostislav A. Belyakov and his first deputy Anatoliy A. Belosvet kept a constant check on the programme.

Mikoyan engineers undertook a massive design effort to create a low-RCS airframe making large-scale use of composites, including major airframe assemblies. A combined flight control system was developed to provide concerted operation of the numerous control surfaces and the vectoring engine nozzles. Meanwhile, other specialised design bureaux participating in the programme were busy defining the architecture of the avionics suite with multiplex data exchange channels, new data presentation/input methods and high-powered new-generation standardised computers. A lot of work was undertaken on integrated avionics, including a new-generation fire control radar, and new types of missiles.

Since the two-class (light fighter/heavy fighter) concept had been abandoned in favour of a 'one size fits all' approach, the 'multi-function' bit of the MFI's name became extremely important. In practice this meant the fighter was to have both air-to-air and air-to-ground capability without one compromising the other. True, the Soviet fourth-generation fighters (the MiG-29 and Su-27) could

Mikoyan MFI and Sukhoi S-37

Above: This full-scale forward fuselage section of the 1.42 mounted on a rocket-powered trolley was used for ejection seat trials at GosNIPAS in Faustovo near Moscow. The ejection seat, complete with dummy, is in the foreground.

Below: The *izdeliye* **1.44 demonstrator nearing completion at the Mikoyan OKB's experimental shop.**

carry free-fall bombs, unguided rockets and other kinds of air-to-ground weapons. However, their strike capability was rather limited due to lack of appropriate targeting systems and other equipment associated with the air-to-ground role. (It was this shortcoming that later led to the development of upgraded *Fulcrums* (MiG-29M, MiG-29SMT, MiG-29UBT) and *Flankers* (Su-27SK, Su-35, Su-37, Su-30MK, Su-35UB) having true air-to-ground capability.)

The first set of blueprints of the MFI was released in 1986, even before the advanced development project (ADP) was reviewed by the Powers That Be. Meanwhile, aerodynamic research continued in TsAGI's wind tunnels and at the Soviet Air Force Research Institute named after Valeriy P. Chkalov (NII VVS – Na**ooch**no-is**sled**ovatel'skiy insti**toot** Vo**yen**no-voz**doosh**nykh sil) in Akhtoobinsk near Saratov in southern Russia. NII VVS utilised large-scale radio-controlled models taken aloft by a helicopter and then released to glide to the ground. Special attention was paid to stability and handling at extreme AoAs, spin recovery characteristics and other modes lying at the limits of the fighter's flight envelope.

The tests at NII VVS proceeded amid extreme security measures. The test drops were carefully timed to hours when US surveillance satellites were not hanging over the area; nevertheless, the gliding models were painted in a green/yellow camouflage – just in case. A NII VVS employee who witnessed the tests recalled that the recovery team was required to retrieve the model and get it out of sight within minutes after landing. The models were rigged with sensors and a data link system transmitting air data to ground stations. The data, as well as photos, cine and video footage shot during the tests, were passed on to the Mikoyan OKB and appropriate sections of TsAGI, NII VVS and the Flight Research Institute named after Mikhail M. Gromov (LII – **Lyot**no-is**sled**ovatel'skiy insti**toot**) for analysis. This, in turn, led to changes in the aircraft's appearance.

Theoretical research and tests of gliding models with mechanical flight controls confirmed that the fighter could remain stable and controllable at AoAs up to 60°. Until then this had been considered impossible for statically unstable aircraft with no autostabilization system designed for extreme flight modes.

As noted earlier, the *izdeliye* 1.42 – or simply 1.42, as it was often called – was a lot different from Soviet (Russian) fourth-generation fighters. Unlike the MiG-29 and Su-27, it had wings with straight leading edges. There were no leading-edge root extensions (LERXes); instead, the vortices energising the airflow over the wings at high alpha were formed by the canard foreplane attachment beams. The thickness and position of these beams with respect to the wings were selected by trial and error. Early project configurations of the 1.42 had conventional all-movable canards with an unbroken leading edge, but a dogtooth was later added to generate extra vortices. The dogtoothed canards were unique; the only other aircraft to have this feature so far was the 'MiG-35', a much-modified MiG-29, which turned out to be a hoax.

Multi-mission MiG

Another view of the 1.44 in the final assembly shop.

(Incidentally, the 1.42 paralleled the development of the MiG-23 in this respect. The original MiG-23S *Flogger-A* had a straight wing leading edge at maximum sweep. From the MiG-23M *Flogger-B* onwards a dogtooth was introduced on the movable outer wings and augmented by a second dogtooth on the wing gloves of the ultimate MiG-23MLD *Flogger-K*, greatly enhancing manoeuvrability.)

Gradually the outlook of the aircraft crystallised. A curious feature of the 1.42 was the multitude of control surfaces adapting the fighter's aerodynamics to all flight modes.

Various ways of internal weapons carriage were studied in order to reduce the 1.42's RCS while enabling it to cruise at supersonic speed with a normal weapons load (ie, with no external stores). At one time Mikoyan engineers considered a dorsal weapons bay with hydropneumatic rams ejecting the missiles during launch. This arrangement offered certain advantages, simplifying target lock-on and missile launch during high-G manoeuvres. On the down side, it caused certain engineering problems, not to mention the fact that arming the aircraft would be extremely complicated, as standard missile loading equipment would be unusable. Eventually the engineers chose a more conventional arrangement with a ventral weapons bay in the centre fuselage.

The RCS was reduced by canting the vertical tails outward some 15° and minimising the gaps between the control surfaces and the rest of the airframe. On the other hand, some features (the fuselage spine and the ventral fins) certainly did not help stealth. Of course Mikoyan engineers were aware of this, hence the use of these features shows the advantages they confer outweigh the disadvantages. For instance, the ventral fins are unique in that their aft portions are movable, acting as supplementary rudders, which should enhance directional control in some flight modes.

Special mention must be made of the fighter's combined flight control system. In addition to the regular control surfaces it includes the high-lift devices (two-section leading-edge flaps and two-section flaperons) and the vectoring engine nozzles. All of them receive pilot inputs by means of a digital fly-by-wire (FBW) control system. This constantly monitors the behaviour of the statically unstable aircraft in all flight modes, helping to prevent an irrecoverable departure from controlled flight and reducing pilot workload.

Mikoyan MFI and Sukhoi S-37

Above: Raptor 4001, the first production F-22A, during a test flight.

Below: This early-production Su-27UB (08 Blue) was converted into the LL-UV (PS) TVC testbed. The port engine is equipped with a boxy extension incorporating a 2-D vectoring nozzle.

As already mentioned, the 1.42 was to have state-of-the-art avionics, including a powerful phased-array fire control radar and a rear warning radar (RWR). Besides triggering the aircraft's active ECM equipment upon detecting enemy fighters in the rear hemisphere, the RWR could guide short-range AAMs launched backwards (opposite to the flight direction) to these targets! This 'tail protection' capability had been incorporated in the R-60/R-60M (NATO AA-8 *Aphid*) and R-73 (AA-11 *Archer*) 'dogfight AAMs' developed by NPO Molniya (Lightning).

The companies developing avionics for the MFI were facing numerous tasks, all of which were equally important. Computers with artificial intelligence had to be created, along with numerous databases. A system for in-advance time-scale computing of strike mission profiles had to be developed. Various methods of 'filtering' and sorting incoming information (for instance radar data) had to be devised in order to negate the adverse effect of haze over the combat area on the aircraft's targeting systems, select priority threats while identifying and tracking multiple air and ground targets. Finally, the algorithms of using radar data in the integrated WCS had to be developed.

Multi-mission MiG

The growing number and complexity of the tasks to be solved by the MFI's avionics dictated the approach to the on-board digital computing system, which was designed as an integrated system with common data processing resources and task distribution rather than just a number of interconnected processors, each doing its own task. Computer hardware for the Soviet fifth-generation fighters was developed by the Angstrom enterprise in Zelenograd, the 'Science City' a short way north of Moscow.

At an early stage of the fighter's development it became obvious that the MFI was a lot different from the American fifth-generation fighters. For instance, the Mikoyan fighter had a variable ventral air intake from the start, whereas the F-22 had non-adjustable two-shock lateral intakes optimised for supersonic cruise and the rival Northrop/General Dynamics YF-23 had non-adjustable dorsal intakes. Soviet aerodynamicists believed a ventrally located intake offered certain advantages during vigorous manoeuvres, minimising the danger of an intake stall during high-G turns and high-alpha flight. Also, the tail-first layout maximised lift and the canards performed a pitch damping function at critical AoAs. By comparison, the F-22 and YF-23 utilised a more conventional layout with trapezoidal wings and stabilators.

Preliminary calculations showed that the Mikoyan MFI would have a higher combat efficiency than both the rival Sukhoi S-32 FSW project described later, the F-22 and the European tail-first fighter projects – the British Aerospace EFA (European Fighter Aircraft, now Eurofighter Typhoon), SAAB JAS-39 Gripen and Dassault Rafale.

NPO Lyul'ka-Saturn made considerable progress on the AL-41F new-generation afterburning turbofan, working with TsIAM to design the engine and integrate it into the MFI's airframe. Full-scale development had been initiated by a joint directive of the Soviet Council of Ministers and Communist Party Central Committee as early as 1986. The OKB's founder Arkhip Mikhailovich Lyul'ka had retired by then, and his deputy Viktor Mikhailovich Chepkin became General Designer.

The AL-41F had been specifically designed for a Mikoyan fighter from the outset. This was no small task. The specified engine performance could only be attained by increasing specific engine loads (ie, increasing the overall engine pressure ratio while reducing the number of compressor stages). This called for the use of new structural materials; another prerequisite was the use of an all-new full authority digital engine control system (FADEC) integrated with the aircraft's control system.

MiG-25PD '306 Blue' (c/n N84042680, f/n 0306), the *izdeliye* 84-20 testbed for the MFI's AL-41F engine.

Mikoyan MFI and Sukhoi S-37

As noted in the previous chapter, the engines were required to give the aircraft sustained supersonic cruise capability. In practice this meant cruising at supersonic speed with the engines at full military power (supercruise mode). In comparison, the best fourth-generation fighters could exceed Mach 1 in level flight only by using afterburners, which increased fuel consumption dramatically, limiting supercruise time to just ten or fifteen minutes. (A notable exception is the MiG-31 *Foxhound* heavy interceptor; its Solov'yov D-30F-6 afterburning turbofans are optimised for prolonged supersonic cruise.) The Soviet Air Force's general operational requirement (GOR) for fifth-generation fighters stated that the aircraft was to cruise at supersonic speed for much longer periods, engaging the afterburners only when sharp manoeuvres or rapid acceleration were needed.

The AL-41F was designed from the outset as a thrust-vectoring engine to suit the MFI's ultra-manoeuvrability requirements. Originally Mikoyan engineers envisaged two-dimensional (2-D) nozzles as fitted to the McDonnell Douglas F-15S/MTD (STOL/Maneuverability Technology Demonstrator). This arrangement allowed pitch-only TVC but was both more 'stealthy' and easier to build than an axisymmetrical convergent-divergent vectoring nozzle. Hence NPO Lyul'ka-Saturn concentrated on a 2-D nozzle, developing an axisymmetrical nozzle in parallel as a 'belt-and-braces' policy.

In 1989 NPO Lyul'ka-Saturn and the Sukhoi OKB converted a Su-27UB *Flanker-C* combat trainer coded 08 Blue into a propulsion technology (TVC) testbed. (Unlike Western military aircraft which have *serials* allowing positive identification, since 1955 Soviet/CIS military aircraft have two-digit *tactical codes* which are usually simply the aircraft's number in the unit which operates it. Three-digit codes are usually allocated to development aircraft, often tying in with the construction number (manufacturer's serial number) or fuselage number (line number), though some SovAF transports which were previously quasi-civil have tactical codes matching the last three digits of the former civil registration.) A long boxy extension with a wedge-shaped rear end incorporating a 2-D nozzle was grafted onto the port engine, replacing the standard nozzle. Hence the aircraft was referred to as LL-UV (PS) (for *le***ta**yuschchaya labora***tor***iya s oopravl***ya***yemym **vek**torom [*tyaghi*], **plos**koye **sop**lo – TVC testbed with a 'flat', ie, two-dimensional nozzle). The standard axisymmetrical nozzle on the starboard engine was retained; in contrast, the F-15S/MTD had two vectoring nozzles.

Tests confirmed that the vectoring nozzle was working as it should, giving the expected improvement in agility. However, the 2-D nozzle proved impractical, as the temperature distribution in the jetpipe was unsatisfactory (some parts of the jetpipe where it changed from circular to rectangular cross-section got excessively hot, which could result in a burnout). Lyul'ka-Saturn had to equip the AL-41F with an axisymmetrical vectoring

The 1.44 prototype jacked up for landing gear retraction tests at Mikoyan's experimental shop.

Multi-mission MiG

The first open-air photos of the 1.44 taken in the summer of 1994.

nozzle; the design was finalised in 1991 and incorporated in the ultimate configuration of the MFI.

The AL-41F incorporated a number of revolutionary technologies (including powder metallurgy) and made use of advanced materials, including composites and new alloys. Lyul'ka engineers had gone to great lengths to reduce the engine's heat and radar signature and refine its aerodynamics. All of this resulted in much-improved performance in virtually every aspect as compared to existing fighter engines (the Lyul'ka OKB's previous product, the AL-31F afterburning turbofan powering the Su-27). For instance, turbine temperature increased by 12% while weight/thrust ratio reached an impressive 0.09 versus 0.125 for the AL-31F. The thrust/frontal area ratio, another important factor, was also improved. As compared to its predecessor the AL-41F had fewer components; the high-pressure turbine had monocrystalline blades making use of a new blade cooling concept. One of the main targets NPO Lyul'ka-Saturn had to meet was a reduction in operating costs by some 25%.

As with the aircraft it was to power, development of the AL-41F proceeded quite briskly at first. When the Soviet Union disintegrated in late 1991, however, state funding for the MFI programme was reduced dramatically and then, a few years later, dried up almost completely. NPO Lyul'ka-Saturn was forced to continue development as a private venture. Nevertheless, the company managed to build a few dozen prototype engines which underwent bench testing at Lyul'ka-Saturn's own test facility and at TsIAM.

In 1993 LII commenced initial flight testing of the AL-41F on one of its Tupolev Tu-16LL *Badger-A* engine testbeds. The development engine was carried under the bomber's fuselage in a special nacelle which was extended from the bomb bay before starting. Later the engine was installed in a different testbed – a modified MiG-25PD *Foxbat-E* interceptor

19

Mikoyan MFI and Sukhoi S-37

More photos of the 1.44 taken in mid-1994. The moment of the rollout was carefully chosen to prevent the aircraft from being seen by surveillance satellites. After a quick photography session the aircraft was hangared until late 1998.

(*izdeliye* 84D) – in place of the port Tumanskiy R15BD-300 afterburning turbojet. Coded 306 Blue (c/n N84042680, f/n 0306) and redesignated *izdeliye* 84-20, this aircraft made more than 30 test flights, some of them at high altitudes and supersonic speeds. Despite the difference in thrust between the turbofan and the standard turbojet (about 17,700 kgp/39,020 lb st versus 11,200 kgp/24,691 lb st in full afterburner) which had its adverse effect on the aircraft's handling, the MiG-25PD testbed reached speeds in excess of Mach 2. In-flight shutdown and restarting was tried successfully, among other things. The tests yielded a huge amount of valuable data and led Lyul'ka-Saturn to make certain changes to the engine.

The presence of multiplex data exchange channels in the fifth-generation fighter's avionics

Multi-mission MiG

Left: A fine study of an F-22A during a test flight with the internal weapons bays open. The Mikoyan MFI utilises the same approach to weapons carriage.

suite necessitated the introduction of all-new data recording equipment integrated into the suite and controlled by the aircraft's mainframe computer. To this end NPO *Preebor* (Instrument) in St. Petersburg and another avionics enterprise designed the Gamma-1106 recorder for the 1.42 – the first of its kind in Russia. Apart from ordinary wires, the recorder could use fibe-optic communications. It was tested successfully on a modified MiG-29 *Fulcrum-A* owned by the Mikoyan OKB and known as 'aircraft 211' or *izdeliye* 9.21 (11 Blue, c/n unknown, f/n 1601). Another unique data storage and analysis system created for the 1.42 was the ASIS-2000, its on-board components undergoing trials on several avionics testbeds.

Stealth had become one of the key words in fifth-generation fighter design, and of course this applied to the Soviet fighter of the 21st century as well. Besides the usual ways of attaining this goal – use of radar-absorbent materials and coatings and designing the airframe in such a way as to minimise the RCS, Soviet scientists worked on technologies the likes of which did not exist anywhere in the world. For instance, in a radical departure from traditional stealth technologies the research centre named after Mstislav V. Keldysh devised a revolutionary 'stealthogenic' system. The system used wisps of plasma formed by pencils of electromagnetic rays

Below: This is how the aviation press first saw the Mikoyan 1.44 or MFI on 12th January 1999.

Mikoyan MFI and Sukhoi S-37

from special generators installed on the aircraft; the plasma absorbs radio waves, reducing the aircraft's RCS approximately 100 times.

Thus by the end of the 1980s the Soviet aircraft industry had accumulated the know-how enabling it to create a true fifth-generation fighter – a fighter that would surpass the best Western aircraft in its class, including the Lockheed Martin F-22A Raptor.

In 1988 the Mikoyan OKB received a specific operational requirement (SOR) for the MFI (*izdeliye* 1.42) multi-role fighter. The first complete set of blueprints was issued the following year. In 1991 the advanced development project of the MFI passed the Air Force's review with flying colours. Next thing the OKB started issuing manufacturing drawings and other technological documents to be passed on to the production factory which would build the new MiG. (Unlike the Western world, in the Soviet Union/CIS the design bureaux/aircraft companies did not have their own factories, apart from experimental facilities for prototype construction. When a new aircraft was ordered into production, this took place at one of the large factories controlled by MAP (though most of them had strong ties to this or that OKB). Only recently have the Russian design companies and aircraft manufacturers started to merge into Western-style corporations.)

Meanwhile, the OKB's experimental plant (MMZ No. 155) and MAP aircraft factory No. 21 in Gor'kiy (now called *Nizhego**rod**skiy avi-atsee**onn**yy za**vod** 'So**kol**'* – Nizhniy Novgorod aircraft factory 'Falcon') were gearing up to build the prototypes of the MFI. This was a totally new kind of aeroplane, which meant advanced structural materials had to be introduced, many new technologies mastered and the number of composite parts (including major airframe assemblies) greatly increased.

Mikoyan's engineering staff did an immense design job on the fighter's systems (first and foremost the combined FBW control system); lots of software was written for the MFI's computers, and test and data recording/data link equipment prepared. Numerous test rigs and 'iron birds' were built by Mikoyan and TsAGI for verifying the flight controls, electrics, hydraulics, fuel system and air conditioning system. Many pilots had a chance to 'fly' the 1.42 long before it actually took to the air. NPO Avionika (Avionics), which was responsible for the unique flight control system, and NPO **Rod**ina (Mother-land), which manufactured the all-new control surface actuators, contributed a lot to the design process.

The air intakes, control surfaces and weapons placement were defined and refined over and over again, among other things. One of the features on the MFI says that four of the six consecutive overall configurations of the fighter were tested as gliding scale models at NII VVS. Meanwhile, the ejection seat was tested at the State Research and Test Range for Aircraft Systems (GosNIPAS) in Faustovo near Moscow, using a 1.42 forward fuselage installed on a rocket-powered trolley.

As a first step towards full-scale testing of the MFI, the Mikoyan OKB decided to build a technology demonstrator. Bearing a separate manufacturer's designation, *izdeliye* 1.44, this aircraft would perform the initial flight test programme, verifying the chosen aerodynamic layout and the combined FBW control system. It would also be used to measure the RCS and verify some of the fighter's systems.

Still, as the saying goes, man supposes, God disposes. The collapse of the Soviet Union and ensuing turmoil caused the mighty Soviet aircraft industry to break down, with a lengthy recovery process following. Unfortunately, the design bureaux which were the brains of the industry were the hardest hit. The perpetual reorganisations at Mikoyan in 1991-2000 and the changes of management as the company was shuffled from one government structure to another inevitably had a detrimental effect on Mikoyan's military programmes – including the MFI.

After 1992 funding of the MFI programme became almost non-existent. In fact, the almost completed 1.44 demonstrator sat for several years minus control actuators because ANPK (*Aviatsee**onn**yy na**ooch**no-proiz**vod**stvennyy **kom**pleks* – Aviation Research & Production Complex) MiG could not pay NPO Rodina for them! This, in turn, caused the first flight date to slip indefinitely. Still, the company's experimental factory supervised by V. S. Pavlov managed to build a full-scale mock-up and sections of the 1.44 airframe intended for static tests. Together with NAZ Sokol and other production plants acting as subcontractors it made preparations for prototype construction, manufacturing the tooling etc.

Coded 01 Blue, the prototype of the 1.44 demonstrator (still lacking some equipment items) was trucked to Mikoyan's flight test facility at LII in Zhukovskiy south of Moscow in early 1994. In summer the aircraft was rolled out for the first official company photographs to be taken (with all due precautions to prevent it from being 'seen' by US surveillance satellites). After that the prototype remained hangared for the rest of the year, carefully positioned in such a way as to prevent unauthorised personnel from seeing it by mischance, as even the fighter's appearance was highly classified.

Multi-mission MiG

The ground test programme got under way at the end of the year. In late December 1994 the still-incomplete 1.44 made its first high-speed run with Mikoyan chief test pilot Roman Taskayev at the controls.

Then the test programme was halted because, as already mentioned, ANPK MiG had no money to purchase the missing components. Seeing this, Mikoyan's arch-rival, the Sukhoi OKB, seized the chance to beat the competitor and fly their fifth-generation fighter first. Sukhoi were better off financially, having sold several Su-27SKs and Su-27UBKs to China and Vietnam, along with a batch of Su-30Ks for the Indian Air Force. Part of the proceeds from these sales was diverted to the completion of Sukhoi's fighter technology demonstrator originally known as S-32 but then redesignated S-37.

Sukhoi achieved their goal: the S-37 prototype entered flight test ahead of the Mikoyan MFI on 25th September 1997. Several modifications were made after the preliminary flight tests which took place in the autumn of 1997 and the spring of 1998. Still, try as they would to attract the Russian Air Force's attention to the Berkoot, Sukhoi had virtually no success. For one thing, the Mikoyan MFI had been ordered by the VVS from the start and funded by the Ministry of Defence. Unlike the 1970s when the MiG-29 and Su-27 were developed to complement, rather than compete with, each other, the Russian military wanted a single fifth-generation aircraft, a jack of all trades – simply because they could not afford two aircraft developed by competing bureaux. Small wonder that the MoD wanted to see the result of those investments. Secondly, Mikoyan's design concept suited the Air Force better than the unorthodox forward-swept wing S-37.

Meanwhile, in the mid-1990s the USAF had completed the flyoff between the two ATF contenders, the Lockheed Martin YF-22A and the Northrop YF-23A. Lockheed Martin won and the YF-22A was ordered into production as the Raptor. The first production F-22As commenced flight tests at Edwards AFB, California, in September 1997.

In June 1995 MAPO MiG's Deputy General Designer Anatoliy A. Belosvet created a minor sensation at the 41st Paris Aerospace Salon, announcing that the MiG MFI prototype might be unveiled at the MAKS-95 airshow due to take place in Zhukovskiy on 22nd-27th August. The aircraft received a new coat of paint for the occasion; however, the Ministry of Defence refused to declassify the fighter and the prototype stayed behind firmly closed doors in a hangar during the show. Nevertheless, the painting effort was not in vain – the MFI prototype was demonstrated to the MoD top brass and some members of the Russian cabinet of ministers in the said hangar. (MAPO = *Moskovskoye aviatseeonnoye proizvodstvennoye obyedineniye* – Moscow Aircraft Production Association named after Pyotr V. Dement'yev. Apart from the Mikoyan OKB, it included two production factories – MMZ No. 30 at Moscow-Khodynka and the Lookhovitsy Machinery Plant near Moscow (both building Mikoyan fighters), the NPO Klimov (OKB-117) engine design bureau in St. Petersburg etc.

At the press conference on occasion of the MiG-AT advanced trainer's rollout which took place on 1st March 1996, MAPO MiG General Director Vladimir Kooz'min said the MiG 1.44 might commence flight testing 'six months from now', given proper funding. The company made another try to show the new fighter at the MAKS-97 airshow (19th-24th August 1997) but the scenario was repeated – the General Headquarters said no.

Left and below: These first official photographs of the 1.44, taken by Igor' Korotchenko, were published by the Russian daily *Nezavisimaya Gazeta* on 24th December 1998.

Mikoyan MFI and Sukhoi S-37

Multi-mission MiG

This page and opposite page: The 1.44 at the official rollout in Zhukovskiy on 12th January 1999.

Mikoyan MFI and Sukhoi S-37

Above and right: The 1.44 taxies along LII's runway on 12th January 1999 with Mikoyan CTP Vladimir Gorboonov at the controls.

Multi-mission MiG

Left: Vladimir Gorboonov climbs out of the 1.44's cockpit.

Below: The spectacular taxying run completed, Gorboonov prepares to answer the questions of the press.

In the late 1990s ANPK MiG was in dire financial straits and the programme had to be mothballed. The company addressed numerous government agencies, seeking support, but to no avail. Only when Mikhail V. Korzhooyev was appointed General Director and General Designer at Mikoyan did things start changing for the better. The MFI was 'dusted off' and A. A. Belosvet was put in charge of the preparations for the flight tests.

When Gheorgiy A. Sedov was appointed counsellor to ANPK MiG's General Designer in 1998, Yuriy P. Vorotnikov succeeded him as MFI project chief. At this time the anti-Mikoyan lobby supported by some members of the Russian government launched an attack on the new top executives of ANPK MiG; a spate of critical publications and scathing comments appeared in the Russian media. Nevertheless, the embattled company made renewed attempts to speed up the MFI programme during this period; for example, a State Duma (lower house of the Russian parliament) delegation was invited to inspect the 1.44 prototype at LII.

By then everyone, including the Russian military, was aware that further delays in fifth generation multi-role tactical fighter development could cause the programme to be abandoned altogether. This, in turn, would damage the nation's defence capability immeasurably, as Russia would fall far behind the USA in aviation technology. Thus in the final weeks of 1998 ANPK MiG finally managed to break through the walls of secrecy and red tape, persuading the Powers That

27

Mikoyan MFI and Sukhoi S-37

Multi-mission MiG

Be to reveal the MFI's outlook to the public. On 24th December the *Nezavisimaya Gazeta* daily published a brief news item about the fighter accompanied by several photos.

12th January 1999 was a special day in world aviation history: the Mikoyan 1.44 prototype was formally rolled out at last. The ceremony was attended by top-ranking Russian officials, including Defence Minister Igor' Sergeyev, VVS/PVO C-in-C Col. Gen. Anatoliy Kornookov, his deputy Lt. Gen. Yuriy Klishin and Presidential advisor on aviation matters Yevgeniy Shaposhnikov. Other guests at the ceremony included Minister of Economy Andrey Shapoval'yants, Metropolitan (the Russian Orthodox Church's equivalent of a bishop) Kirill of Smolensk and Kaliningrad, foreign military attaches and

Above and opposite page: These photographs of the 1.44, were taken during when the aircraft first left the hangar in the summer of 1994.

Left: The 1.44 was the centre of attention of press photographers and TV camera crews for several hours during the 12th January rollout ceremony.

Mikoyan MFI and Sukhoi S-37

Russian and foreign media representatives. Before the invited guests were allowed to examine the MFI 'up close and personal', the aircraft taxied up to them along LII's runway with new Mikoyan CTP Vladimir Gorboonov at the controls; this trick was intended to show that the prototype was ready to commence flight tests.

Interestingly, the first photos of *izdeliye* 1.44 to appear outside Russia were published by *Aviation Week & Space Technology* on 11th January, one day before the official roll-out! A selection of official Mikoyan OKB photos appeared on the Internet shortly afterwards. All of them were the original photos taken back in the summer of 1994. The upper views published in *AW&ST* were taken from the roof of the hangar at Mikoyan's flight test facility in Zhukovskiy. One can only guess how the American magazine laid hands on these pictures, but it seems quite probable that it was a carefully organised 'leak' intended to arouse interest in the MFI before the official debut. (This is because, given the lack of official information and two frustrating 'no-shows' in Zhukovskiy, the Western world was growing increasingly sceptical about the Mikoyan 1.42, as the fighter was known to the West, some industry experts even presumed that the programme was 'dead and buried' because of defence budget cuts.)

So, what does Mikoyan's fifth-generation fighter look like? The MFI is a single-seat heavy fighter utilising, for the first time in Russia, the twin-tailed close-coupled canard layout. While resembling both the F-22A and the Eurofighter Typhoon in certain respects, it still has characteristic Mikoyan traits. The aircraft has mid-set delta wings with a straight leading edge and no LERXes. The wings feature almost full-span leading-edge flaps and large two-section elevons. The large canards mounted immediately aft of the cockpit have a dogtooth near the roots.

Above and below: Front and three-quarters rear views of the 1.44 demonstrator.

Multi-mission MiG

Above and below: Numerous aviation experts and journalists attended the rollout ceremony.

Mikoyan MFI and Sukhoi S-37

Right: The dogtooth on the canard foreplanes of the 1.44 is evident in this view; moreover, a slight deflection of the canards creates the false impression the canards have a double dogtooth!

Below: This view emphasises how high the 1.44 sits over the ground.

The twin fins are spaced wide apart and canted sharply outwards in a manner reminiscent of the F-22. The fins are attached to long slender oval-section booms outboard of the engines and augmented by fairly large ventral fins (which, unlike the fins, are not canted). As already mentioned, for the first time in fighter design practice the aft portions of the ventral fins are movable, augmenting the conventional rudders. Unusually, small inset elevators, or 'elevatorettes', are incorporated between the fins and engine nozzles to assist the canards.

It can be noted that with fourth-generation fighters, the Su-27 family has ventral fins while Mikoyan discarded them after using them briefly on early *Fulcrum-As*. With fifth-generation fighters, it is vice versa; Mikoyan used ventral fins and Sukhoi did not!

The aft-hinged canopy is outwardly similar to that of the MiG-29 but opens in a different way, rising slightly on two pairs of parallel arms and then tipping aft. It is followed by a rather fat fuselage spine which may be further enlarged later on to accommodate additional fuel and/or avionics.

Multi-mission MiG

The 1.44 is powered by two Lyul'ka-Saturn AL-41F afterburning turbofans. As already mentioned, the engines have axisymmetrical convergent-divergent nozzles with thrust vectoring in both pitch and yaw planes. Unusually, the inner petals of the nozzle are covered with a heat-resistant ceramic material, hence their light tan colour. The AL-41F, which recently entered production at the Rybinsk engine factory, gives the aircraft both ultra-manoeuvrability throughout the speed range and extended supersonic cruise capability.

The engines are located very close together and breathe through a Eurofighter-style common boxy intake under the forward fuselage with adjustable horizontal flow control ramps and a movable lower lip to improve high-alpha performance. The intake is divided by a splitter and transforms into two S-ducts. Here, Mikoyan engineers have succeeded in making a virtue out of necessity: while introduced primarily to circumvent the internal weapons bay, the S-ducts also add stealth, being coated with RAM. (Speaking of which, the 1.44 demonstrator has no provision for

Above: Among other things, the 1.44 demonstrator differs from previous Mikoyan fighters in having an unusual quasi-triangular section nose.

Below: The vertical tails are carried on widely spaced booms tipped with dielectric fairings.

Mikoyan MFI and Sukhoi S-37

Upper three pictures: Sequence of stills from a Mikoyan video capturing the 1.44's first takeoff on 29th February 2000. Note the orange efflux indicating a high nitrous oxide content.

Lower three pictures: The 1.44 demonstrator comes in to land and touches down.

weapons, the weapons bay being occupied by test equipment.)

Landing gear design is straightforward, with a twin-wheel nose unit (similar to that of the MiG-29, though much shorter) retracting aft into the air intake splitter and levered-suspension main units retracting forward into the fuselage sides. The Mikoyan MFI appears to sit slightly lower over the ground than its Sukhoi competitor. The reason may be that the S-37's nose gear unit is positioned ahead of the air intakes and the danger of foreign object damage (FOD) is greater, forcing Sukhoi to take preventative measures. Mikoyan claim that the MFI will have better field performance than current fighters; the tough landing gear typical of Russian fighters will undoubtedly contribute to this.

Like the F-22A which is made largely of titanium and steel alloys, the *izdeliye* 1.44 demonstrator makes relatively modest use of carbonfibre reinforced plastic (CFRP) and other composites which account for some 30% of the total weight. This is due to purely technological reasons; among other things, it is difficult to mate composite structures with parts made of traditional alloys in places where large structural loads are applied. Besides their obvious advantages, composites also have a few weaknesses. Low repairability is one; it is virtually impossible to repair damaged composite structures in service conditions, which means large airframe components may have to be replaced. Hence on the MFI composites are used for the canards, wing skin panels, landing gear doors and various access panels.

Mikoyan spokesmen have stated many times that the MFI incorporates a measure of stealth technology. Russian experts claim that the fighter's unconventional layout, coupled with the use of RAM, screening of highly reflective parts (such as engine compressor faces) and internal weapons carriage have resulted in an RCS comparable to that of the F-22A thanks to the use of RAM, internal weapons stowage and other structural features. If this is true, Mikoyan have scored a point, since the Russian fighter is clearly larger than the Raptor. This may indeed be true, considering that Mikoyan have considerable experience with RAM. Much attention has been paid to reducing the MFI's heat signature.

The MFI is equipped with a fifth-generation pulse-Doppler fire control radar often referred to as N-014, indicating it is a product of NPO Fazotron (aka NIIR – the Radio Research Institute). This is a phased-array radar designed for beyond visual range (BVR) air-to-air combat and has multiple target attack capability. Mikoyan spokesmen

Multi-mission MiG

said at the rollout ceremony that the radar of the future production-standard aircraft will track up to 20 targets while guiding AAMs to six priority threats. The dielectric nose fairing of '01 Blue' is remarkably small, however, suggesting that no radar is fitted. The aircraft also features a comprehensive ECM/ESM suite, part of which is located in the vertical tail attachment booms tipped by dielectric fairings; more aerials are housed in the wingtips, fin caps and the front ends of the ventral fins, which are dielectric.

It should be noted that the future fully-fledged version of the MFI (*izdeliye* 1.42) will differ from the *izdeliye* 1.44 demonstrator in a number of respects. First of all, the air intake will be redesigned *à la* Mikoyan Ye-8 experimental fighter of 1962, with a V-shape in plan view and vertical flow control ramps incorporated in the splitter. This arrangement is more 'stealthy'; besides, Mikoyan engineers were somewhat apprehensive about the 1.44's intake design, fearing it might cause the engines to surge or flame out during sharp manoeuvres (testing intake performance was part of the idea with building the demonstrator). Secondly, the combat version will have the intended fire control radar, which will necessitate a change in the shape of the nose (the 1.44 demonstrator has a flat-bottomed nose of quasi-elliptical cross section). Thirdly, *izdeliye* 1.42 will feature a flight refuelling probe. Finally, the wing planform will be slightly different.

Generally the appearance of the MFI is nothing revolutionary from a Western point of view. However, Russian aviation experts point out that its structure and aerodynamics have been carefully designed and should meet the designers' expectations. Mikoyan cite the fighter's long range, high top speed (estimated as about Mach 2.35) and low IR signature even in cruise mode as its strong points.

Throughout 1999 the company prepared the demonstrator for flight tests. The missing control actuators were purchased and installed at last; all systems were checked and numerous engine runs made. Still, the first flight date kept slipping, causing a new wave of caustic comments from the 'anti-MiG lobby'. Meanwhile MAPO MiG was renamed once more, becoming RSK MiG (*Rosseeyskaya samolyotostroitel'naya korporahtsiya* – Russian Aircraft Corporation) on 8th December 1999, the Mikoyan OKB's 60th birthday.

Finally, on 23rd February 2000 (Russian Armed Forces Day!) preparations for the maiden flight of the 1.44 began in earnest. On that day the fighter made another high-speed run and rotation, getting the nosewheels off the ground briefly. Then the technical council

Above, centre and below: More video footage of the 1.44's maiden flight. The landing gear stayed down on that occasion; a MiG-29 acted as a chase plane.

Lower two pictures: During the second flight on 27th April 2000 the landing gear was cycled for the first time.

Mikoyan MFI and Sukhoi S-37

Above and below: Three more views of the 1.44 during the 12th January 1999 rollout.

36

Multi-mission MiG

of the Artyom I. Mikoyan Engineering Centre (as ANPK MiG was renamed when Nikolay F. Nikitin succeeded Mikhail V. Korzhooyev as General Designer) convened to decide whether it was safe to fly the aircraft. The verdict was yes, but nothing could be done until LII reached an identical conclusion; the go-ahead from LII came a few days later.

At 11:25 AM Moscow time on 29th February 2000 the Mikoyan 1.44 made its long-expected maiden flight at the hands of Distinguished test pilot (an official grade reflecting experience and expertise) Vladimir Gorboonov. The flight was extremely brief, lasting a mere 18 minutes; the fighter landed at 11:43 AM after climbing to 1,000 m (3,280 ft) and making circling the airfield twice at 500 to 600 km/h (270 to 324 kts). Gorboonov said later that 'the aircraft was docile – there were no surprises, though this is obviously a totally new kind of aircraft'.

The first flight took place amid extremely tight security measures bringing vivid recollections of the Cold War when everyone in the Soviet Union was paranoid about secrecy. Very few 'outsiders' were allowed to witness the event, and photos and video footage taken that day were not passed to the media. It was not until two weeks later, when a video of the first flight had been edited by the company's PR section and personally approved by Nikolay F. Nikitin, that ORT (the government TV channel) showed a brief sequence on the evening news. Actually, no information would probably have been released at all, had it not been for the fact that the 1.44 was the first brand-new Mikoyan aircraft to fly for the last 20 years (!); the event clearly meant a lot to the company which needed a boost of morale very much indeed. Besides, Mikoyan's new chief executive was not an active supporter of the MFI programme.

Still, the MFI (or, to be precise, the 1.44) finally **did** fly. Whatever the results of that brief flight, it started the trials of an aircraft of a completely new kind by Mikoyan standards.

The second test flight took place on 27th April. On this occasion the landing gear was cycled for the first time and the aircraft climbed to 2,000 m (6,561 ft) during the 22-minute flight. As of this writing, however, no further flights have been reported. This may indicate that the first flight has revealed some design shortcomings and it is back to the drawing board for now.

Above: The layout of the 1.44 is such that the vertical tails shield the engine nozzles, helping to reduce the aircraft's heat signature.

Below: The adjustable supersonic air intake is located under the forward fuselage.

Mikoyan MFI and Sukhoi S-37

RSK MiG General Designer Nikolay Nikitin says many of the features used on the 1.44 demonstrator will be used in the future fifth-generation fighter.

Multi-mission MiG

Mikoyan 1.44 in detail

The following provisional description of *izdeliye* 1.44 is based on the information available as of this writing.

Type: Twin-engined heavy tactical fighter technology demonstrator utilising the statically unstable close-coupled tail-first layout. The airframe makes use of lightweight high-strength aluminium-lithium alloys (35% of the dry weight), steel and titanium alloys (30%), CFRP and other composites (about 30%). Other structural materials (glass, Perspex, rubber etc.) account for 5% of the dry weight. The design incorporates numerous stealth features reducing the aircraft's radar and heat signature.

Fuselage (lifting body): The fuselage is designed in such a way as to minimise surface area and cross-section area. To this end the engine air intakes are located in a single fairing; the engines are also located as close together as possible. The fuselage contributes a sizeable amount of lift. The forward fuselage has quasi-elliptical cross section changing to almost rectangular further aft and then back to elliptical. The small dielectric nosecone terminates in an unusual forked pitot but this is part of the test instru-

Above: The 1.44's air intake has dorsally-mounted horizontal flow control ramps and an adjustable lower lip for high-alpha flight.

Below: The two-piece canopy affords good cockpit visibility.

Mikoyan MFI and Sukhoi S-37

Above, left and right: The 1.44's cropped-delta wings feature dielectric wingtip fairings for ESM antennas.

Above: The 1.44's rear section.

Above: The canard foreplanes.

Below, left and right: The vertical tails and ventral fins.

Multi-mission MiG

mentation (the upper pitot is a backup and will be removed later on). The centre fuselage incorporates the main fuel tanks.

The variable supersonic air intake located under the forward fuselage is raked, with rectangular cross-section at the inlet. It has dorsally-mounted horizontal flow control ramps and a movable lower lip to improve high-alpha performance. To prevent boundary layer ingestion the intake is installed at a short distance from the flat forward fuselage undersurface so that the upper lip acts as a boundary layer splitter plate; a V-shaped fairing spilling the boundary layer connects the upper lip to the fuselage. The intake is divided by a vertical splitter; each half transforms into a circular-section S-duct for the respective engine going up to circumvent the weapons bay. This shields the engine compressor faces, significantly reducing RCS.

The pressurised cockpit is enclosed by a canopy consisting of two parts – a one-piece curved windscreen made of birdproof Triplex glass and an aft-hinged rear portion. The latter rises slightly on two pairs of parallel arms and then tips aft when opened; this unusual arrangement reduces the force required to open the canopy manually in the event of hydraulics failure. The canopy is followed by a rather fat fuselage spine which terminates in a boattail fairing between the engine nozzles; this probably houses brake parachutes.

Foreplanes: Cantilever shoulder-mounted all-moving structures of composite construc-tion. Leading-edge sweep 58°, trailing-edge sweep 23°; large dogtooth near the roots for energising the airflow over the wings at high AoAs.

Wings: Cantilever mid-set delta wings with a straight leading edge and no LERXes; leading-edge sweep 52°, trailing-edge sweep 0°. Prominent booms mounting the vertical tails and housing ECM/ESM equipment are incorporated into the wings at approximately quarter-span; the trailing edge inboard of these is extended far aft. The wings have almost full-span leading-edge flaps, large two-section elevons outboard and small inset elevators, or 'elevatorettes', inboard of the vertical tail attachment booms; the trailing-edge device actuators are enclosed by prominent ventral

Above: Another view of the 1.44's vertical tail.

Below: The main (left) and nose (right) landing gear units.

Mikoyan MFI and Sukhoi S-37

Above and below: The nozzles of the AL-41F turbofans are coated with special heat-resistant ceramic tiles on the inside, hence their light tan colour.

fairings. Hardpoints for three external stores pylons are provided under each wing. The wingtips are formed by large dielectric fairings for ECM/ESM antennas.

Tail unit: Basically vertical tail surfaces only (apart from the abovementioned 'elevatorettes'). Twin fins of trapezoidal planform with very slight forward sweep on the trailing edges, augmented by large ventral fins. The vertical tails are attached to the widely spaced wing booms mentioned earlier; the fins are canted 14° outwards to reduce the aircraft's RCS in side elevation while the ventral fins are not.

The fins incorporate large inset rudders, while the aft portions of the ventral fins are movable, augmenting the conventional rudders. The fin caps and the fixed front portions of the ventral fins are dielectric, housing navigation and communications aerials.

Landing gear: Hydraulically-retractable tricycle type. The semi-levered suspension nose unit with twin 620x180 mm (23.6x6.3 in.) wheels retracts aft into the air intake vertical splitter; due to the limited space available the wheels protrude slightly beyond the fuselage contour and the twin lateral nose gear doors are suitably bulged. The levered suspension main units with single 1,030x350 mm (40.55x13.77 in.) wheels retract forward to lie in the centre fuselage sides, the wheels rotating around the legs in the process; each mainwheel well is closed by tandem doors. All three units have oleo-pneumatic shock absorbers.

Powerplant: Two Lyul'ka-Saturn AL-41F afterburning turbofans rated at about 17,700 kgp (39,020 lb st) in full afterburner. The engines have supersonic convergent-divergent axisymmetrical nozzles having thrust vectoring in pitch and yaw planes; the nozzles' inner petals are faced with heat-resistant ceramic tiles. The aggregate thrust of two AL-41Fs in full afterburner gives the 1.44 a thrust/weight ratio around 1.33 (with a normal TOW, that is).

The engine features a full authority digital engine control system (FADEC) system. Dry weight is 1,585 to 1,600 kg (3,494 to 3,572 lb), which amounts to a weight/thrust ratio of 0.09. As of now the AL-41F's guaranteed life until the first overhaul is 1,000 hours and the service life of the nozzle's movable parts is 250 hours, though this is to be increased to 500 hours.

Control system: Combined fly-by-wire (FBW) control system with multiple backup which includes both conventional control surfaces and thrust-vectoring control (TVC). Roll control is provided by two-section elevons, pitch control by the all-movable canards, 'elevatorettes' and TVC, and directional control by main and auxiliary rudders and TVC. The engines' FADEC is also integrated into the flight control system.

Multi-mission MiG

Left: The 1.44's forward fuselage.

Avionics and equipment: The avionics suite of the future production-standard aircraft (*izdeliye* 1.42) will comprise a weapons control system (WCS), a navigation suite, a communications suite and an ECM/ESM suite.

The *WCS* will be built around a fifth-generation pulse-Doppler phased-array multimode fire control radar (possibly the Fazotron N-014). The radar is designed for BVR air-to-air combat and can track up to 20 aerial targets while guiding AAMs to six priority threats. A rear warning radar (RWR) is also to be installed. However, the 1.44 demonstrator has no radar, since this aircraft was built primarily for verifying the close-coupled canard layout and the MFI's required manoeuvrability.

The WCS will also include an optoelectronic targeting system consisting of an infra-red search & track unit/laser rangefinder (IRST/LR) and a helmet-mounted sight (HMS). These enable the pilot to track targets and aim missiles in poor visibility conditions without switching on the radar and revealing himself to the enemy. Furthermore, the HMS increases targeting efficiency in a dogfight, offering 'point and shoot' capability; the pilot can provide target information to the IRST/LR and missile seeker heads by simply turning his head.

The *navigation suite* will include an inertial navigation system (INS) and a global positioning system (GPS), a short-range radio navigation (SHORAN) and automatic approach/ landing system and other equipment normally fitted to tactical aircraft. The *ECM/ESM suite* will include an active jammer with antennas located in the wingtip fairings and vertical tail attachment booms to give 360° coverage.

The cockpit features a bioadaptive indication system allowing the pilot to select the required quantity of information and data presentation mode on the multi-function displays (MFDs). Realistic presentation of the tactical situation, coupled with interactive controls,

Above and left: The booms carrying the vertical tails terminate in large dielectric fairings, indicating that a comprehensive ESM suite (possibly including a rear warning radar) was envisaged.

43

Mikoyan MFI and Sukhoi S-37

Above and below:
The planned production version of the 1.44 was to feature an internal weapons bay housing missiles but this is faired over on the demonstrator.

enable the pilot to manage the fighter's systems and weaponry more efficiently.

The *flight avionics* include a unique system called KSL (*kontrol' sostoyahniya lyotchika*) which continuously monitors the pilot's physical condition. The system not only alerts the pilot that he is pulling Gs which are critical for him but takes over and brings the aircraft into straight and level flight automatically, should the pilot experience G-*loc* (G-induced loss of consciousness).

Crew escape system: The 1.44 is equipped with a variable-geometry zero-zero ejection seat designed by NPP Zvezda (Star, pronouncd *zvezdah*) under Guy Il'yich Severin. Variable geometry in this instance means that seat incline can be adjusted in flight, enabling the pilot to absorb higher G loads.

Armament: As already mentioned, the 1.44 demonstrator lacks armament; still, it has the internal weapons bay and wing pylon hardpoints of the real thing. The production-standard *izdeliye* 1.42 will have one 30-mm (1.18 calibre) single-barrel internal cannon of an unspecified type; for added stealth the cannon port will be closed by a special door when the cannon is not selected 'on' by the pilot.

Air-to-air missiles of varying range (specially developed for the MFI) will be carried on ejector racks in the internal weapons bay; the AAM types have not been reported to date. Air-to-surface weapons and drop tanks will be carried on six underwing pylons. In addition to specially-developed new-generation air-to-surface missiles, the MFI will be able to carry nearly all ASMs, unguided rockets and bombs currently used by Russian tactical aircraft. It should be noted, however, that normally the aircraft is to carry internal weapons only, since high-drag external stores increase RCS and preclude supersonic cruise.

Aerospace publications have reported details of advanced Russian AAMs. For example, the R-77M active radar homing medium-range AAM developed by the Vympel (Pennant) OKB is effective at up to 90 km (48.6 nm) range. It differs from the basic R-77 (RVV-AE/NATO AA-12 *Adder*), in having folding rudders for internal carriage. The 21-kg (46-lb) warhead is an annular pack of small shaped charges (for maximum penetration) and is detonated by a laser proximity fuse. Another spinoff of the R-77 is the solid-fuel ramjet-powered RVV-AE-PD (*povyshennaya dahl'nost'* – extended range) capable of destroying enemy aircraft up to 160 km (86.48 nm) away. Both versions can be launched in reverse direction for protection against pursuing enemy fighters.

The new highly agile R-73M 'dogfight AAM' has a two-range IR seeker head with a 180° field of view; its detection range and sensitivity has been doubled as compared to the original R-73 (AA-11). The R-73M has a 60-km (32.4-nm) maximum effective range and can destroy targets flying as low as 5 m (16 ft). The missile can make 12-G turns to keep up with the target's evasive manoeuvres; at the terminal guidance phase it goes for the centre of the target's fuselage instead of the engine nozzle which is the hottest part of the airframe, thereby maximising kill probability.

As of this writing the official target performance figures of the Mikoyan 1.42 fighter and ithe 1.44 demonstrator, remain classified. Very few figures have been quoted, and these are by no means 100% accurate. What has been reported is that the fighter is some 20 m (65 ft 7.4 in.) long, with a wingspan of some 15 m (49 ft 2.55 in.). Normal takeoff weight and MTOW have been reported as approximately 30 tons (66,137 lb) and 35 tons (77,160 lb) respectively; top speed is estimated as Mach 2.35 and cruising speed as Mach 1.4 to 1.6.

Multi-mission MiG

Left and below: In the spring of 2001 the chief executives of RSK MiG decided to carry on with the 1.44's trials programme after the aircraft had been suitably modified.

Mikoyan MFI and Sukhoi S-37

Top view of the *izdeliye* 1.44 experimental aircraft.

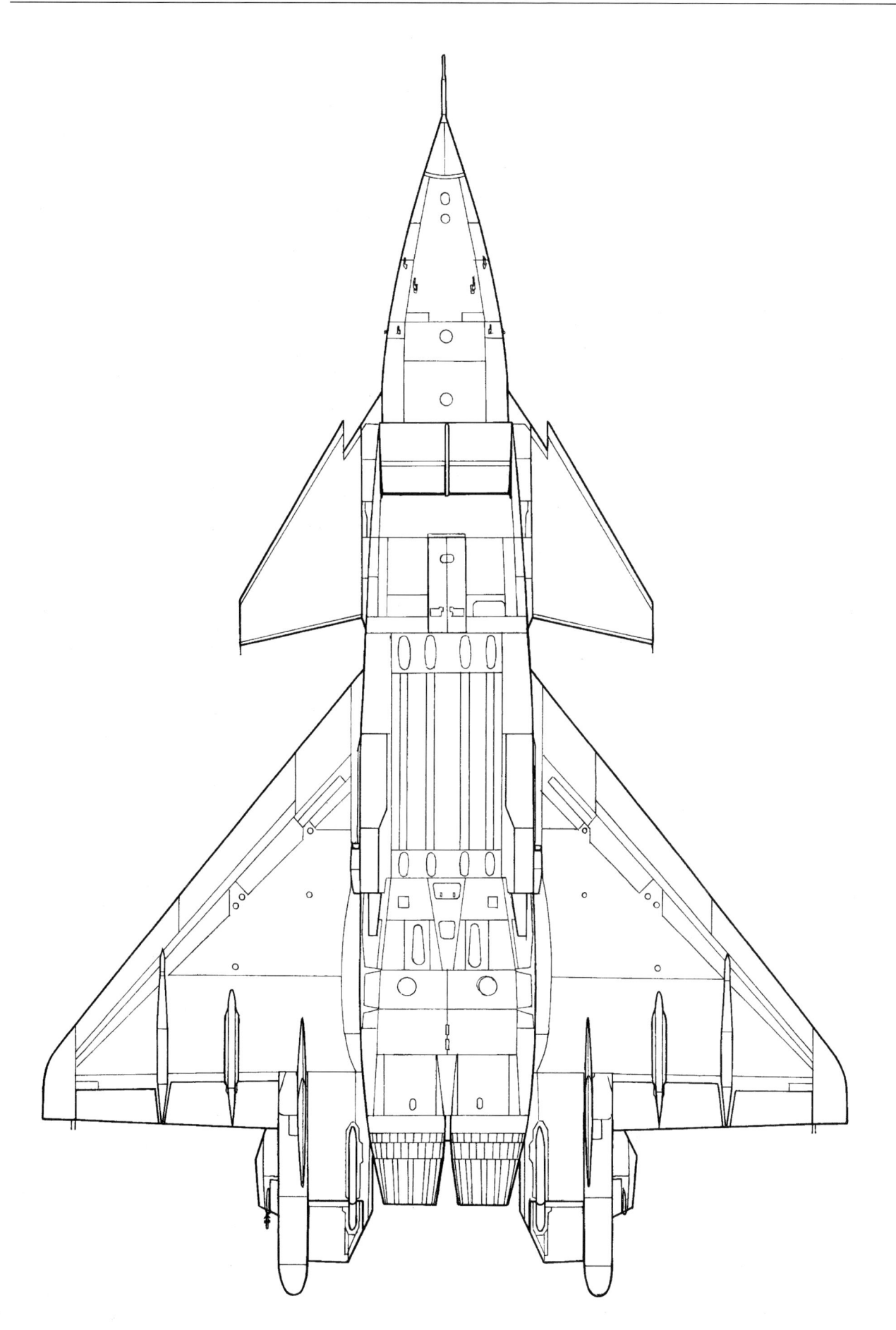

Multi-mission MiG

Bottom view of the *izdeliye* 1.44 experimental aircraft.

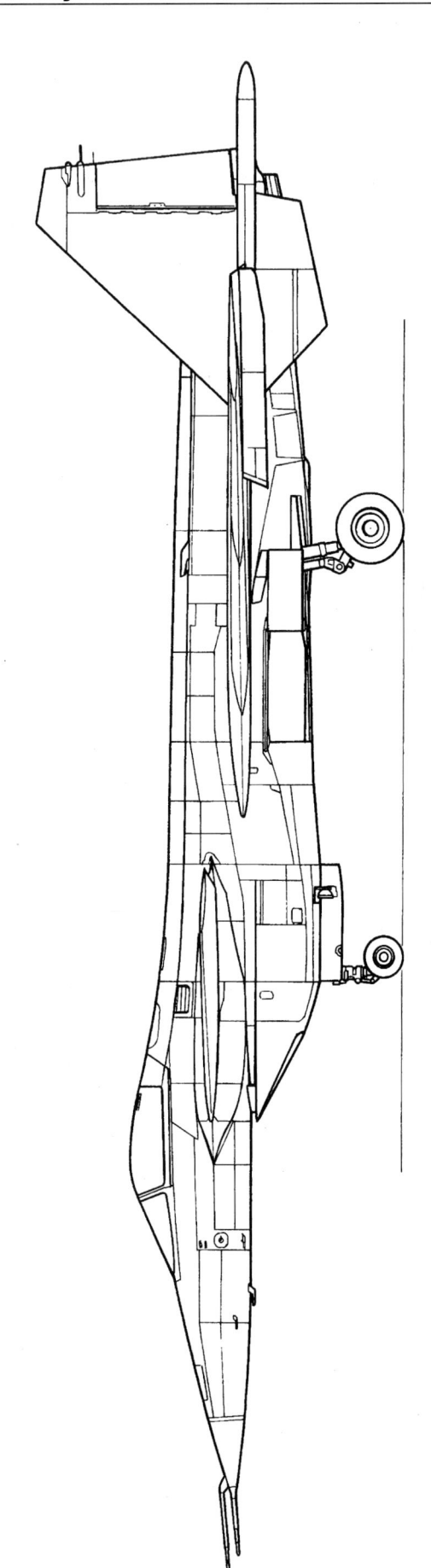

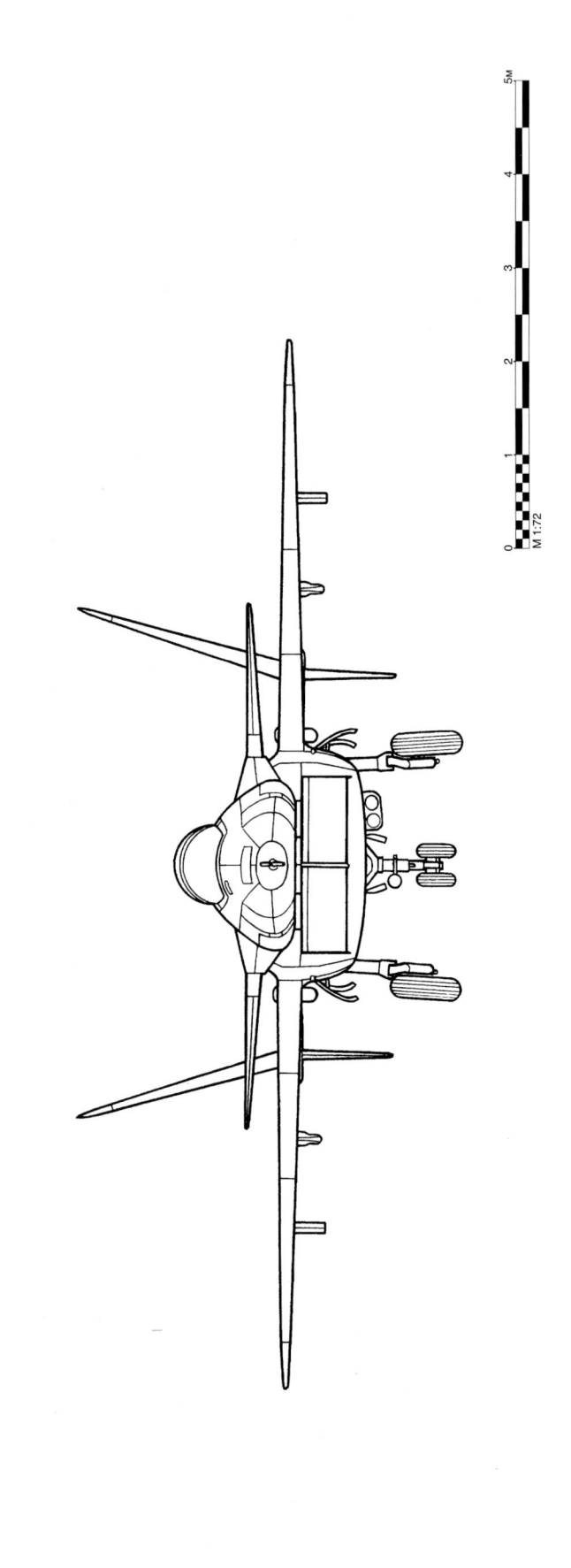

Mikoyan MFI and Sukhoi S-37

Port and front views of the *izdeliye* 1.44 experimental aircraft.

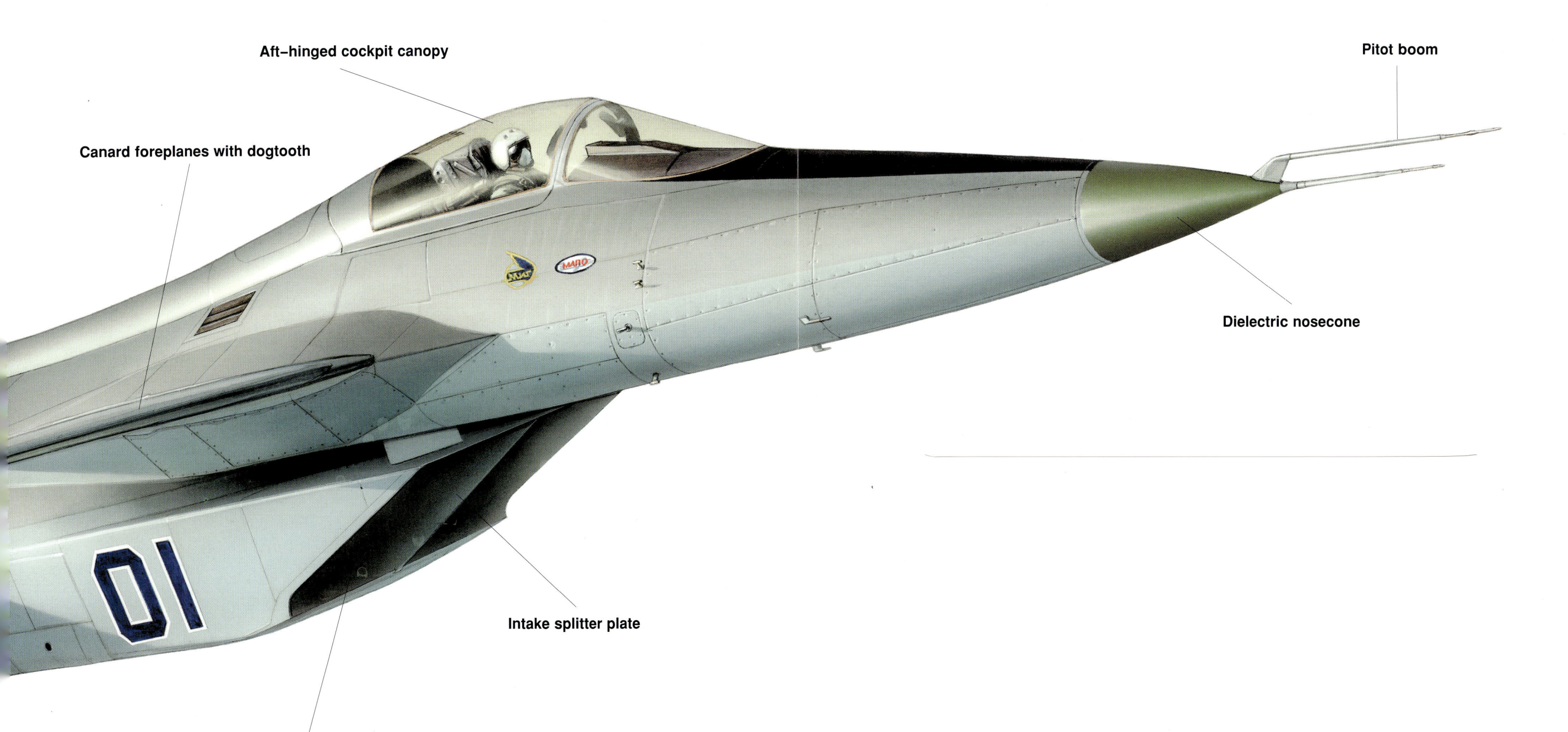

- Aft-hinged cockpit canopy
- Pitot boom
- Canard foreplanes with dogtooth
- Dielectric nosecone
- Intake splitter plate
- Adjustable supersonic air intake

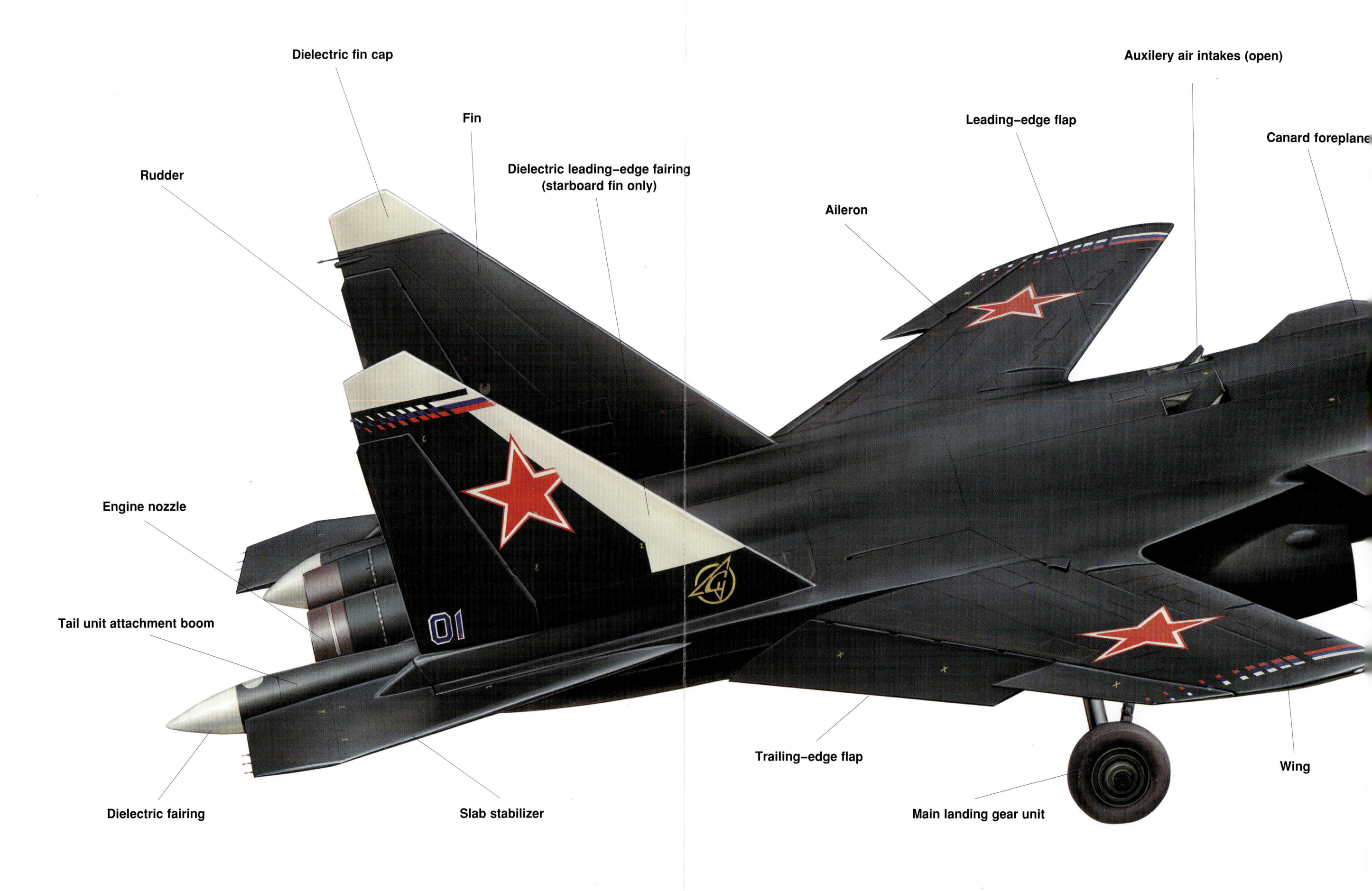

- Dielectric fin cap
- Fin
- Dielectric leading-edge fairing (starboard fin only)
- Auxilery air intakes (open)
- Leading-edge flap
- Canard foreplane
- Rudder
- Aileron
- Engine nozzle
- Tail unit attachment boom
- Trailing-edge flap
- Wing
- Dielectric fairing
- Slab stabilizer
- Main landing gear unit

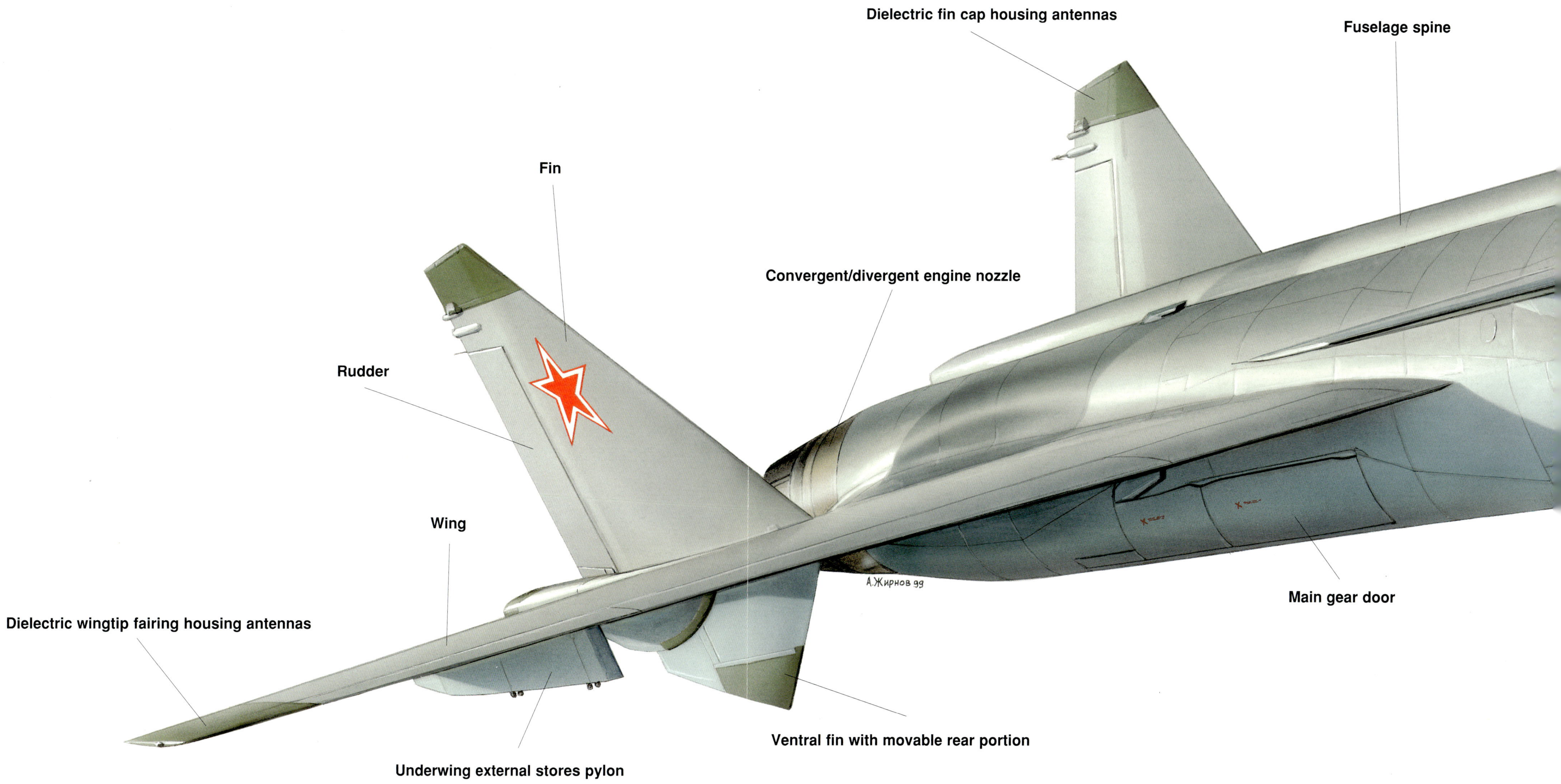
Dielectric fin cap housing antennas
Fuselage spine
Fin
Convergent/divergent engine nozzle
Rudder
Wing
А.Жирнов 99
Main gear door
Dielectric wingtip fairing housing antennas
Ventral fin with movable rear portion
Underwing external stores pylon

- Leading edge root extension
- Aft-hinged cockpit canopy
- Fixed curved windshield
- Main pitot head
- IRST fairing
- Communications aerial
- Air data boom
- Radone
- Backup pitot head
- ECM antenna fairing
- Fixed-area air intake
- Main gear door
- Twin-wheel nose landing gear unit

S-37
Proud Bird of Prey

Mikoyan MFI and Sukhoi S-37

As already noted, the Sukhoi OKB's fifth-generation fighter developed under the I-90 programme had forward-swept wings. This layout based on aerodynamic research by TsAGI and SibNIA offered extreme agility; the aircraft would be capable of controlled flight at AoAs of 90° or more. (It should be noted that the ultramanoeuvrability requirement applied not only to the Soviet I-90 programme but to the ATF programme as well. The Americans, however, ran into serious technical problems and had to sacrifice agility as a trade-off for solving them.)

Analysis of post-World War II military conflicts shows that, despite the advent of medium-/long-range AAMs and powerful airborne radars, close-in dogfighting remains practically inevitable. Today's long-range AAMs are by no means a 100% 'kill' guarantee. This was illustrated by the Gulf War of 1990-91 when US Navy Grumman F-14 Tomcats and McDonnell Douglas F/A-18 Hornets were in action against Iraqi aircraft; the GM/Hughes AIM-120 AMRAAM and Raytheon AIM-7M Sparrow medium-range AAMs and GM/Hughes AIM-54 Phoenix long-range AAMs fired by the American fighters often missed their targets. Furthermore, the development of advanced ECM systems and incorporation of stealth technologies into modern fighters further reduces the efficiency of such weapons.

Air war tacticians claim that when large groups of fighters clashed during past armed conflicts, neither side could gain a decisive advantage in a short time when attacking at medium range. Even in BVR combat between aircraft having similar speed envelopes and comparable weapons, the pilot who manages to point his fighter at the enemy first has an advantage ('first sight, first shot, first kill'). This is especially true when the pilot has to fire consecutively upon several targets in different sectors of airspace; the faster he manages to point the aircraft at the next target and get a lock-on, the better he can use the dynamic capabilities of his weapons.

Thus present-day combat tactics require a fighter to have the highest possible turn rate, as well as the widest possible speed range within which the weapons can be used. This means the aircraft's aerodynamics and systems must enable it to change attitude and trajectory rapidly. All of this caused the military on both sides of the Iron Curtain to place high demands on a fifth-generation fighter's agility.

As already mentioned, the Soviet Air Force officially selected the Mikoyan OKB and the delta-wing, canard layout for the MFI programme. Nevertheless the Sukhoi OKB chose to carry on with the forward-swept wing MFI project at its own risk; this decision was taken largely thanks to General Designer Mikhail Petrovich Simonov who realised that the project held promise. Later, current S-37 project chief Sergey Korotkov explained this 'private venture' as follows: 'Russian defence spending was slashed in the early 1990s, still the [Sukhoi] OKB decided to continue development [of the FSW fighter]. We were convinced that it was necessary to keep up advanced aircraft design technologies. Indeed, the loss of just a single component in the system of combat aircraft generation change inevitably causes a nation to lose the capability to design and build state-of-the-art fighters. This is exactly what happened to Germany, Great Britain and Japan which are now a generation behind Russia, the USA and France.'

What made Sukhoi engineers go for the highly unconventional FSW layout? Forward-swept wings are known to give a number of advantages over the classic swept-wing layout. These are:
– a much better lift/drag ratio during manoeuvres, especially low-speed ones;
– a better L/D ratio and longer range in subsonic cruise mode thanks to lower trim drag;
– higher lift and hence a bigger relative payload;
– better control characteristics at low subsonic speeds and better field performance;
– better operating conditions for the high-lift devices and hence higher efficiency, which again improves field performance;
– a lower stalling speed which enables the aircraft to fly safely at lower speeds;
– excellent spinning characteristics (the aircraft is virtually spin-proof);

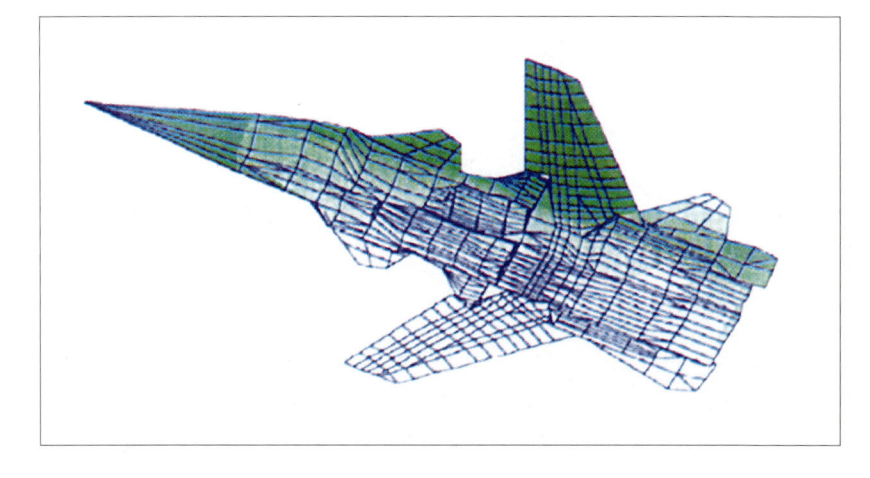

S-37: Proud Bird of Prey

– bigger internal fuselage volume, especially at the wing/fuselage joint (this facilitates provision of an internal weapons bay, thereby helping stealth);

– the FSW layout is suited to a wide range of mission profiles, as the aircraft is equally stable throughout the speed range.

Early attempts to use forward-swept wings on military aircraft date back to the 1940s. The world's first FSW aircraft was the Junkers Ju 287 bomber, the first prototype of which (the four-jet Ju 287 V1, coded RS+RA) entered flight test on 16th August 1944. In its intended production form (Ju 287A) it was to have a top speed of 815 km/h (440.5 kts). Two more German experimental FSW bombers, the six-engined Junkers EF 131 (Ju 287 V2) and the twinjet Junkers EF 140, fell into Soviet hands at the end of the war and were completed and test-flown in the Soviet Union.

In the immediate post-war years the Soviet Union started its own FSW research programme, testing the feasibility of using such wings on fast agile combat aircraft. In 1945 LII tasked aircraft engineer Pavel Vladimirovich Tsybin with developing a series of experimental rocket-powered gliders intended for researching the aerodynamics of future jet fighters. The gliders would be towed to high altitude by an aircraft and then reach transonic speeds in a dive, accelerated by the solid-fuel rocket booster. The third of these gliders (designated LL-3) had wings swept forward 45° at quarter-chord. Tested in 1947, the LL-3 attained 1,150 km/h (621.62 kts) or Mach 0.95.

The advantages conferred by forward sweep could not be used in practice at the time, however, because forward-swept wings were prone to divergence. As the wings bent under aerodynamic loads the angle of attack (and hence lift) on the outer portions increased; this in turn increased the air loads, causing further deformation. The aircraft became statically unstable at certain speeds and AoAs; worse, the aerodynamic loads

The EF140 or 'aircraft 140' forward-swept wing development aircraft designed by Junkers engineers in Germany but completed in the USSR after the war.

Pavel V. Tsybin's LL-3 experimental rocket-powered FSW glider.

Mikoyan MFI and Sukhoi S-37

The Grumman X-29A FSW proof-of-concept aircraft

would grow as airspeed increased, eventually exceeding the wings' structural strength limits. Given the technologies and structural materials of the time, it was impossible to design sufficiently stiff forward-swept wings without incurring an unacceptable weight penalty which negated any aerodynamic benefits.

The idea was revived only in the mid-1970s when new lightweight and strong composite materials (namely CFRP) came on the scene. As the suitability of composites for airframe design was explored, aerodynamicists developed a special method of calculating wing stiffness. The wing divergence problem could be solved by arranging the stiffness axes in such a way as to eliminate twisting as the wings flexed; this was done by using composite structures with carefully arranged fibres for optimum wing stiffness distribution.

Coincidentally R&D establishments in the USA and the Soviet Union began initial studies of a fifth-generation fighter's outlook. Calculations by US aviation experts showed that an FSW derivative of the F-16 would have a 14% higher turn rate, a 34% longer combat radius and 35% better field performance.

In 1981 the Grumman Company began development of the Model 712 (X-29A) FSW demonstrator. Two prototypes were built; flight tests began on 14th December 1984. However, for reasons unknown US companies undertook no further work in this direction; one of the X-29As was transferred to NASA as an aerodynamics research aircraft while the other one is in storage.

American fifth-generation fighters make use of conventional swept wings. A major shortcoming of such wings is that the wingtips stall first, and at relatively small angles of attack. As the aircraft makes manoeuvres and the AoA increases further, airflow separation inevitably spreads over the entire wing surface, reducing lift and ultimately causing the aircraft to stall. Conversely, the tip stall problem is designed out of forward-swept wings; the root portions stall first, which means the ailerons remain effective even at high alpha.

Besides, on an FSW aircraft the greater part of wing lift is generated by the inner wing portions; this reduces the bending load on the wings, making a higher aspect ratio possible. This, in turn, minimises induced drag when the aircraft makes manoeuvres with a high lift coefficient; besides, high aspect ratio wings help to achieve longer range.

S-37: Proud Bird of Prey

It should be noted that forward-swept wings give a lower RCS in the forward hemisphere as compared to conventional swept wings. The USA put this phenomenon to good use; the only FSW aerial vehicle to reach quantity production was the AGM-129 strategic air-launched cruise missile carried by the Boeing B-52 Stratofortress. The choice of layout for this weapon was dictated by stealth needs; radar pulses reflected by the wing leading edges were shielded by the missile's fuselage.

Considering all the advantages described above, Sukhoi engineers selected forward-swept wings for their stealthy super-agile fighter which initially bore the in-house designation S-32. Strictly speaking, it was wrong to use this designation, since it already applied to the Su-17 *Fitter-C* fighter-bomber; perhaps it was reused in order to confuse Western intelligence agencies. The aircraft also had an unofficial name, **Berkoot** (Golden Eagle). The design team tried to incorporate the latest know-how developed by the Soviet aviation science and industry, such as the statically unstable aerodynamic layout, new-generation actuators and new technologies of manufacturing large airframe subassemblies.

The nation's finest aviation research centres, TsAGI and SibNIA, participated in shaping Sukhoi's fifth-generation fighter. Among other things, TsAGI undertook wind tunnel tests of an FSW derivative of the MiG-23 (!), while SibNIA contemplated a similarly 'vivisected' Su-27. Changes to the S-32's aerodynamics were made progressively as the number of wind tunnel hours grew.

A wind tunnel model of an FSW MiG-23 derivative developed by TsAGI

Like their colleagues at Mikoyan, the Sukhoi OKB also used high-tech gliding models to check the aircraft's behaviour in free flight. Among other things, they were used to investigate the aircraft's stalling and spinning characteristics and develop stall/spin recovery techniques. Controlled by an on-board computer, the model would attain high angles of attack – and still follow its intended course without going into a spin. The tests revealed that an FSW fighter was capable of sustained high-alpha flight three or four times longer than the Su-27!

Armed with the results of these tests and ongoing R&D programmes, Sukhoi began development of the world's first supersonic combat aircraft with forward-swept wings. This was a truly Herculean task. Apart from the obvious complexity of the FSW project, the company had to work on other programmes in parallel – eg, advanced versions of the Su-27 (super-agile *Flankers* with canards and TVC) which are called 'Generation 4+ fighters'. Interestingly, the Su-27 upgrade and S-32

The Russian Sukhoi Su-37 super-agile fighter

61

Mikoyan MFI and Sukhoi S-37

Above and below: The first prototype of the Su-30MKI super-agile two-seat multi-role fighter (01 Blue)

programmes inevitably influenced each other, both aircraft borrowing structural and equipment items from each other with minimum changes. Thus the FSW fighter demonstrator shows obvious Su-27 lineage, while some advanced systems created for this aircraft found their way to the latest multi-role *Flanker* derivatives – the Su-37 single-seat fighter, Su-30MK and Su-35UB two-seaters.

Almost from the very start the S-32 programme was led by chief project engineer Mikhail A. Pogosyan who contributed a lot to the development effort. General Designer Mikhail P. Simonov supervised and co-ordinated the programme. Despite the fact that the Berkoot was developed as a private venture, Pogosyan succeeded in taking the project to the prototype construction and flight test stages. In March 1998, when Pogosyan was appointed General director of AVPK Sukhoi, his former deputy Sergey Korotkov became the FSW fighter programme's project chief.

(AVPK = *Aviatsee**on**nyy vo**yen**no-pro**mysh**lennyy **kom**pleks* – Aviation Military-Industrial Complex. Besides the Sukhoi OKB, it includes NPO Lyul'ka-Saturn and three factories building Sukhoi fighters: No. 39, or IAPO (*Ir**koot**skoye aviatsee**on**noye proiz**vod**stvennoye obyedi**nen**iye* – Irkutsk Aircraft Production Association), No. 126 in Komsomol'sk-on-Amur and No. 153 in Novosibirsk. The acronym AVPK is rather pretentious and out of place, as the term *voyenno-pro**mysh**lennyy **kom**pleks* applies to the entire defence industry and not to a single enterprise in this field, important though it be.)

Initially the S-32 was to be powered by two Khachatoorov R79M-300 afterburning turbofans rated at 18,500 kgp (40,784 lb st) in full afterburner. This was an uprated version of the Yak-141's 15,500-kgp (34,171-lb st) R79V-300 lift/cruise engine fitted with a new nozzle which could be deflected ±20° in the vertical plane for thrust-vectoring control. Later Sukhoi engineers rejected it in favour of the Lyul'ka-Saturn AL-41F engine – the same as on the rival Mikoyan MFI. The new powerplant gave the Berkoot a thrust/weight ratio around 1.17 at the maximum takeoff weight or 1.67 at normal TOW, guaranteeing excellent performance.

As a 'belt-and-braces' policy in case the AL-41F proved unavailable (or unsatisfactory), the S-32 could be fitted with an adapted version of the Solov'yov D-30F-6M afterburning turbofan powering the experimental MiG-31M interceptor. This engine delivered nearly 20,000 kgp (44,091 lb st) in full afterburner – quite an improvement on the 15,600-kgp

S-37: Proud Bird of Prey

(34,391-lb st) standard D-30F-6 powering the production MiG-31 *Foxhound*. While not guaranteeing the required supercruise capability, the D-30F-6M still offered acceptable performance, allowing stability/handling, performance and structural strength tests to be carried out and the aircraft's main systems to be verified. In a nutshell, it was adequate for research and development purposes.

It should be noted that the S-32 preliminary design project envisaged a unique feature – a common (!) two-dimensional vectoring nozzle for both engines, similar to the experimental nozzle of the LL-UV (PS) testbed. This arrangement, however, provided for pitch-only TVC.

Guy Il'yich Severin, head of NPP Zvezda (Star, pronounced *zvezdah*; NPP = *Naoochno- proizvodstvennoye predpriyahtiye* – scientific and production enterprise), also had a hand in forming the design of Sukhoi's unorthodox fifth-generation fighter. Even when wearing a G-suit, most pilots suffer ill effects when subjected to sustained forces in excess of 4 Gs. Severin proposed a revolutionary adaptive ejection seat which alleviated the G forces considerably. This would enable the S-32 to pull much higher Gs in a dogfight as compared to contemporary fighters, using the potential of the forward-swept wings to the full.

As design work progressed, the engineers discovered that the S-32 was overweight and the chances of reaching the specified performance target were pretty nebulous. At the same time the Air Force revised its requirements, placing even higher demands on the fighter's performance. All of this led Sukhoi to begin a massive redesign which, in effect, resulted in quite a different aircraft, as evidenced by the new designation. In its ultimate form the project was called S-37; the popular name Berkoot was retained.

Preparations for prototype construction began in the late 1980s at the Sukhoi OKB's experimental plant in Moscow and at the Irkutsk aircraft factory. The plan was to build two flying prototypes and a static test airframe, but this had to be limited to two prototypes after 1991 when the Russian defence budget shrank. When the Russian Air Force stopped funding the S-32-turned-S-37 programme altogether, the Sukhoi OKB had to raise money for prototype construction on its own.

Only a single S-37 airframe had been completed by the early 1990s. Like the Mikoyan 1.44, this was not a true combat aircraft but an FSW and ultra-manoeuvrability technology demonstrator. In 1996, however, a desktop model of a projected Soviet FSW fighter – obviously the intended production configuration of the S-32 (S-37) – was demonstrated to the air force top brass, with photos in the aviation press.

AVPK Sukhoi General Director Mikhail A. Pogosyan who was in charge of the company's fifth-generation FSW fighter project for many years.

Left and below: A model of the S-32 fighter with a common 2-D vectoring nozzle

Mikoyan MFI and Sukhoi S-37

Above and below: In the summer of 1997 the S-37 arrived at Sukhoi's flight test facility in Zhukovskiy

Unlike the Grumman X-29A (which is single-engined and has low-mounted canards, a single fin and wing trailing-edge strakes with trailing-edge flaps), the aircraft had twin tails. The high-set canards were augmented by sharply swept stabilators (admittedly smaller than the horizontal tail of conventional fighters but still bigger than the 1.44's 'elevatorettes'); hence the S-37 is often referred to erroneously as a 'triplane' in the Russian popular press. The wings featured wingtip launch rails for AAMs in the manner of the Su-27. Interestingly, an arrestor hook was installed under the rear fuselage, suggesting possible naval use; the Soviet/Russian conventional takeoff and landing (CTOL) shipboard fighter programmes were well advanced by then. However, a possible explanation is that the fighter was designed with land-based arrestor systems in mind, building on the USAF's experience with the McDonnell Douglas F-4C/D/E Phantom II on tactical airstrips during the Vietnam War.

In the spring of 1997 the first prototype S-37 underwent non-destructive static testing at Sukhoi's experimental plant. For the first time in Russia, Sukhoi engineers made use of new methods which allowed the airframe's structural strength limits to be determined precisely without applying loads big enough to cause permanent deformation.

In the summer the prototype (which, like its Mikoyan competitor, was coded 01 Blue) arrived at the company's flight test facility at LII. Taxi trials and high-speed runs commenced in early September. The maiden flight

S-37: Proud Bird of Prey

was originally slated for 24th September 1997 but had to be cancelled when one circuit of the quadruplex FBW control system failed. This problem was quickly fixed and on September 25 the S-37 became airborne at 03:10 PM Moscow time with Sukhoi OKB chief test pilot Igor' Votintsev at the controls. The first flight lasted 30 minutes and went well.

Unlike the Mikoyan 1.44 which wore a light grey air superiority colour scheme, the S-37 was painted flat black overall, except for the radome and other dielectric parts, which were white, and white/blue/red 'go faster' flashes on the wings, fins and air intakes. This unprepossessing finish served to make it look like a silhouette during future airshow performances and hopefully disguise some features which Sukhoi wished to keep secret for a while (including the internal weapons bay). Thus the S-37 was a 'black' aircraft in more senses than one!

Votintsev was pleased with the S-37, noting the aircraft's extreme agility. A Su-30 of LII's *Ispytahteli* (Test Pilots) display team coded 597 White (c/n 79371010102) and flown by the team's leader Anatoliy N. Kvochur acted as chase plane during the Berkoot's first flight.

The second flight reportedly took place on 1st October, though Sukhoi do not confirm this. On 8th October Russian radio news broadcasts said that 'the new S-32 (*sic*) fifth-generation forward-swept wing fighter had entered flight test'. This was the date of the third flight; the fourth followed on 13th October in defiance of superstition. Igor' Votintsev flew the aircraft on all occasions.

Above and below: An APA-5D power cart based on a Ural-375D 6x6 lorry tows the Berkoot to its assigned parking area after a successful test flight.

Mikoyan MFI and Sukhoi S-37

Above and below: During the autumn of 1997 Sukhoi OKB test pilot Igor' V. Votintsev made several test flights in the S-37. The aircraft was painted flat black overall to disguise some design features, including the internal weapons bay.

S-37: Proud Bird of Prey

Five days later, on 18th October, the S-37 was demonstrated statically and in flight to high-ranking Russian MoD and government officials. The day was carefully chosen. Most Russian aircraft design bureaux have facilities in Zhukovskiy. 18th October was Saturday and most of the other companies' employees were off duty, which meant fewer nosy parker neighbours could see what they were not supposed to. On 24th October the *Kommersahnt* (Trader) daily newspaper published the first photo of the enigmatic Berkoot in flight.

So, here comes the question again: what does Sukhoi's fifth-generation fighter look like? The S-37 is a lot different from its Mikoyan counterpart. Firstly, it has three rows of lifting surfaces: mid-set forward-swept wings, shoulder-mounted canard foreplanes and mid-set slab stabilizers. As already mentioned, this layout reduces the aircraft's RCS in the forward hemisphere. Since the stabilators augment the canards for pitch control, the canards are rather smaller than the Mikoyan MFI's. Secondly, the S-37 utilises the integral or blended wing/body (BWB) design used earlier on the Su-27. Thirdly, it has twin fixed-area lateral air intakes. To speed up development and cut development costs some airframe and systems components (such as the cockpit canopy and landing gear) were borrowed from the *Flanker*.

While manufacturing the S-37's airframe, Sukhoi pioneered some new technologies. For instance, wing and fuselage skins were prefabricated from sheet metal as flat parts and then fashioned into double-curvature panels precisely matched with each other. The use of large skin panels (up to 8 m/26 ft 3 in.) resulted in an extremely smooth surface finish and minimised the number of skin fasteners, improving aerodynamics and saving structural weight.

Photos of the unconventional Berkoot demonstrator taken by Sergey Pashkovskiy appeared in many aviation magazines.

Sukhoi OKB chief test pilot Igor' V. Votintsev was the Berkoot's project test pilot.

67

Mikoyan MFI and Sukhoi S-37

Above and below: The aerodynamic layout selected for the S-37 Berkoot not only provides high performance and good agility but reduces the aircraft's radar signature into the bargain.

S-37: Proud Bird of Prey

As previously mentioned, even though Sukhoi's fifth-generation fighter had been designed around the equally new AL-41F thrust-vectoring engine, the proven D-30F-6M was specified as an alternative powerplant. For whatever reasons – perhaps the intended engines were still unavailable at the time, or the company decided that fitting all-new engines to an all-new aircraft would be too big a risk at this stage – the S-37 demonstrator was fitted with modified D-30F-6Ms for the initial flight tests. At a later stage of the trials the Berkoot was to be re-engined with AL-41Fs, which would give it supercruise capability.

Some Russian authors are doubtful that the aircraft's current (provisional) powerplant will allow it to exceed Mach 1 without using afterburners. In reality, however, it probably will. The question should be whether the D-30F-6Ms will enable the S-37 to keep up the specified cruising speed long enough, as the two engines' specific fuel consumption in various modes is of importance here.

Stage 1 of the flight test programme was completed in the spring of 1998. After that, the aircraft was in layup until the end of the year as changes based on the preliminary tests were incorporated. By January 1999 the S-37 had made nineteen flights. More modifications were made after subsequent test flights. The test programme served basically to confirm the advantages offered by forward-swept wings as regards manoeuvrability. Sukhoi's calculations showed that the Berkoot would be at least equal to the F-22A Raptor – and, in some respects, outperform it.

Unfortunately we cannot yet compare the Russian and American 'birds of prey' as regards performance, since the S-37's specifications (including target performance figures) – and the Mikoyan MFI's as well, for that matter – are still classified. However, some educated guesswork can be done at this stage. Aviation experts believe that the difference between the Berkoot's normal TOW and MTOW is about 10 tons (22,045 lb). This extra load may be distributed differently, depending on the mission. Say, if the S-37 is armed with a 3M80 Moskit (Mosquito, aka ASM-MSS) anti-shipping missile which weighs about five tons (11,022 lb), fuel will make up the rest of

By early 1999 Igor' Votintsev had made nearly twenty flights in the Berkoot.

Igor' Votintsev poses with Sukhoi OKB leaders and design staff immediately after the Berkoot's first flight.

Mikoyan MFI and Sukhoi S-37

The S-37 was unveiled to the public on 15th August 1999 during the Aviation Day flypast at Moscow-Tushino. A few days later it took part in the MAKS-99 airshow.

the weight. Knowing that the Su-27's internal fuel load is 9,400 kg (20,723 lb), we may suppose that the S-37's fuel load is at least equal or even bigger, given its FSW layout which maximises the use of internal space. Thus the Berkoot's combat radius is arguably much longer.

During the summer of 1999 the top executives of AVPK Sukhoi decided to demonstrate the Berkoot at the MAKS-99 airshow which took place from 17th-22nd August 1999. Actually the S-37 made its public debut on 14th and 15th August during the traditional Aviation Day flypast at Moscow's Tushino airfield and the preceding rehearsal for the show.

By the opening day of MAKS-99 the aircraft had made 50 flights. It flew daily during the show, streaming picturesque wingtip vortices but showing little else – to the spectators in the public area, that is. It has to be said that Sukhoi's trick with painting the aircraft black failed; when the Berkoot performed, the underside was clearly visible to press photographers standing on the other side of the field! Photos published in the aviation press clearly showed the long doors of the internal weapons bays on the fighter's belly. Interestingly, the engine efflux was bright orange at times, showing a high nitrous oxide content.

As might be imagined, the Berkoot was one of the stars of the show and a big hit with the crowds, not to mention aviation experts and the press. The S-37's unmistakable 'horned' silhouette quickly earned it such nicknames as *chort* (devil) and *rogahtka* (rubber catapult) – and evoked associations with the characteristic threatening gesture of 'new Russian' gangsters which is well known in Russia.

The next stage of the trials programme, which ended in February 2000, included supersonic flights. According to Igor' Votintsev and other Sukhoi OKB staff participating in the programme, the S-37 handles well and is easy to fly above Mach 1. There have been unofficial reports that the aircraft reached Mach 1.3 at this stage.

This is a major step forward for Sukhoi, whose unconventional fighter technology demonstrator is generating considerable interest in the world aviation community. Experience and know-how gained with the Berkoot will be invaluable in developing future advanced combat aircraft.

S-37: Proud Bird of Prey

Sukhoi S-37 in detail

The following provisional structural description of the S-37 is based on the information available as of this writing.

Type: Twin-engined heavy tactical fighter technology demonstrator utilising a statically unstable close-coupled FSW layout with both canard foreplanes and conventional tailplanes. This layout enables dynamic deceleration (by pitching up to AoAs up to 120°) over a wide range of speeds – from minimum controlled flight speed to Mach 1+.

The S-37 incorporates a completely new skin panel manufacturing technology. Wing and fuselage skins are prefabricated from sheet metal as flat parts and then fashioned into double-curvature panels precisely matched with each other. The use of large skin panels (up to 8 m/26 ft 3 in.) produces an extremely smooth surface finish and minimises the number of skin fasteners; this not only improves aerodynamics and saves weight but also reduces the aircraft's RCS.

Composites make up 13% of the dry weight (their share is to be substantially increased later on). The use of advanced composites increases the load ratio by 20 to 25% while increasing service life 1.5 to 3 times as compared to conventional all-metal structures and helping to obtain the required thermal and radio engineering properties.

Top and above: The S-37 taxies at LII, Zhukovskiy, with some of the resident aircraft and the visiting Aero L-39Cs of the Roos' display team in the background.

Below: The Berkoot shortly after take-off.

Mikoyan MFI and Sukhoi S-37

In February 2000 the Berkoot completed yet another stage of the trials programme during which it went supersonic for the first time.

Material waste is reduced to 15%, manufacturing labour intensity is cut by 40 to 60%. The S-37's design incorporates autoadaptive and pre-stressed structures made of advanced composites with specially calculated strength properties. To speed up development and cut development costs some airframe and systems components (such as the cockpit canopy and landing gear) are identical to those of the Su-27M (Su-35).

Fuselage (lifting body): Blended wing/body design, with the fuselage contributing a sizable amount of lift. The fuselage is mainly of aluminium and titanium alloy construction, with 28 large skin panels (mostly chemically milled).

72

S-37: Proud Bird of Prey

The fairly large conical radome tipped by an air data boom with pitch and yaw vanes has a slightly flattened front end with chines acting as vortex generators for better spin resistance. The *forward fuselage* cross-section changes from circular immediately aft of the radome to an inverted trapezoid aft of the cockpit. This, together with the prominent wing LERXes, ensures undistorted airflow and hence smooth engine operation at any AoA.

The pressurised cockpit is enclosed by a large teardrop canopy consisting of two parts – a one-piece curved windscreen made of birdproof Triplex glass and an aft-hinged rear portion. An IRST 'ball' fairing is mounted ahead of the windscreen, offset to starboard à la Su-27M, Su-27K (Su-33) *Flanker-D* and Su-30. L-shaped pitot heads are mounted just aft of the cockpit on either side.

The *centre fuselage* is of basically oval section which transforms into two circular-section engine nacelles side by side with a narrow flattened fairing in between. The wing centre section is integrated into the centre fuselage which also incorporates a weapons bay with two rows of ventral doors side by side. The engine nacelles are flanked by cylindrical booms; curiously, the starboard boom is much longer than the port one. The booms terminate in conical dielectric fairings and may house the rear warning radar and ECM equipment later on.

The large fixed-area air intakes flanking the centre fuselage are of sectoral shape and have large raked boundary layer splitter plates on the inboard side (adjacent to the fuselage) and the upper side (adjacent to the LERXes). The intakes transform into a circular-section S-ducts going up to circumvent

The S-37's cockpit canopy.

Above: A still from a video showing a front view of the Berkoot.

Below: The S-37's centre fuselage.

Mikoyan MFI and Sukhoi S-37

The photos on this page and pages 75-78 show the S-37 taking off from Zhukovskiy during demonstration flights at the MAKS-99 airshow.

S-37: Proud Bird of Prey

Mikoyan MFI and Sukhoi S-37

S-37: Proud Bird of Prey

Mikoyan MFI and Sukhoi S-37

Above: The Berkoot made daily demo flights at MAKS-99, inevitably generating tremendous public interest.

S-37: Proud Bird of Prey

Above: The S-37 begins a spectacular turn to starboard immediately after getting airborne on yet another display session.

Mikoyan MFI and Sukhoi S-37

Above: The S-37 taxies in after a flight. The open dorsal auxiliary intakes are well visible.

S-37: Proud Bird of Prey

Above: Some structural components of the S-37, such as landing gear and cockpit canopy, were borrowed from the Su-27 family to cut development costs and speed up the design process.

Mikoyan MFI and Sukhoi S-37

A bottom view of the S-37 as it passes before the crowd at MAKS-99.

The S-37's aft fuselage and tail unit.

the weapons bay; this shields the engine compressor faces for added stealth. The inlet ducts incorporate small dorsal auxiliary intakes closed by upward-hinged doors; these open automatically in takeoff/landing mode or during vigorous manoeuvres.

Foreplanes: Cantilever shoulder-mounted all-moving structures of trapezoidal planform mounted on wing LERXes. Leading-edge sweep 50°, trailing-edge sweep −16°. The leading edge of each foreplane incorporates a dielectric ECM/ESM antenna fairing.

Wings: Cantilever mid-set forward-swept wings with large curved LERXes (terminating in line with the ejection seat headrest) and trailing-edge strakes which carry the tail unit. Kinked leading edge with 62° sweep on the inner portions and −20° sweep on the outer portions; constant −37° trailing-edge sweep, aspect ratio about 4.5.

Nearly 90% of the wing structure are made of composites. The outer wings with raked tip fairings fold to save hangar space. They incorporate two-section leading-edge flaps, one-piece trailing-edge flaps and ailerons.

Tail unit: Twin vertical tails of trapezoidal planform, structurally similar to those of the Su-27 but much smaller in relative area, since the S-37's aerodynamic layout provides better directional stability and control at high alpha. The widely spaced vertical tails are attached to the wing TE strakes and canted 6° outwards to reduce the aircraft's RCS in side elevation. Each fin incorporates a large inset rudders whose trailing edge protrudes slightly beyond the fin trailing edge; the latter is kinked at the root. The fin caps and the starboard fin leading edge are dielectric, housing navigation and communications aerials.

The differentially movable slab stabilizers (stabilators) of relatively small span and area have an unusual L-shaped planform, the inner portions being a continuation of the wing TE strakes and the pointed outer portions appearing almost as horn balances. Leading-edge sweep 75°, trailing-edge sweep −5°.

Landing gear: Hydraulically-retractable tricycle type; all units retract forward. The

S-37: Proud Bird of Prey

steerable nose unit has twin KN-27 non-braking wheels (ko*leso* netormoz*noye*) with 680x260 mm (26.7x10.2 in.) tyres. The nosewheel well is closed by a single large door hinged to starboard, Su-27 style.

The main units have single KT-156 brake wheels (ko*leso* tormoz*noye*) with 1,030x350 mm (40.55x13.77 in.) tyres; the wheels incorporate brake cooling fans. During retraction the mainwheels rotate through 90° to lie horizontally in the wing roots; this is done by tilting the axles of the main gear pivots outboard and aft. The mainwheel wells are closed by outward-hinged tandem doors. All three landing gear struts have oleo-pneumatic shock absorbers.

Powerplant: Two modified Aviadvigatel' (Solov'yov) D-30F-6 afterburning turbofans rated at about 20,000 kgp (44,091 lb st) in full afterburner, installed in the aft fuselage side by side. Two Lyul'ka-Saturn AL-41F thrust-vectoring afterburning turbofans rated at about 17,700 kgp (39,020 lb st) in full afterburner are to be installed later on.

The basic D-30F-6 has a bypass ratio of 0.57. The engine consists of seven modules, with a five-stage low-pressure (LP) compressor, a ten-stage high-pressure (HP) compressor with variable first-stage stator vanes, a cannular combustion chamber with 12 flame tubes, a two-stage HP turbine, a two-stage LP turbine, an afterburner with four annular flame holders, and a supersonic convergent-divergent axi-symmetrical nozzle. Bleed air valves at 5th and 10th compressor stages.

Control system: Quadruplex FBW control system developed by MNPK Avionika (*Mos-kovskiy* na*ooch*no-proiz*vodstvennyy kompleks* – 'Avionics' Moscow Research & Production Complex). Roll control is provided by ailerons and differential stabilator deflection, pitch control by the all-movable canards and stabilators, and directional control by the rudders (with provisions for TVC later on). The cockpit features a side-stick with limited travel and pressure-sensing throttle levers.

Avionics and equipment: The future production-standard aircraft based on the S-37 demonstrator will have a state-of-the-art avionics suite comprising a weapons control system (WCS), a navigation suite, a communications suite and an ECM/ESM suite. The WCS will be built around a pulse-Doppler phased-array multi-mode fire control radar. It will also include an infra-red search & track unit/laser rangefinder (IRST/LR) installed in a fairing ahead of the windscreen and a rear warning radar (RWR) installed in one of the booms flanking the engines.

Crew escape system: Standard Zvezda K-36DM zero-zero ejection seat installed at a 30° incline to help the pilot tolerate high G loads during manoeuvres. An advanced zero-zero ejection seat enabling safe ejection in inverted flight at low altitude may be installed later.

Armament: The S-37 demonstrator lacks armament, though it has the internal weapons bays of the future combat version. The latter will have one 30-mm (1.18 calibre) Gryazev/ Shipoonov GSh-301 single-barrel internal cannon built into the port LERX; its rate of fire is 1,500 rounds per minute. For added stealth the cannon port will be closed by a special door when the cannon is not selected 'on' by the pilot.

By analogy with the Su-35/Su-37 it appears likely that the combat version will be able to carry long-range and ultra-long-range AAMs. The primary armament, however, will apparently consist of Vympel R-77M (RVV-AE/AA-12 *Adder*) medium-range AAMs with active radar homing optimised for internal stowage. The missile has low aspect ratio wings and folding lattice-like rudders. A faster and longer-range derivative designated RVV-AE-PD and powered by a solid-fuel ramjet has been tested successfully on a Su-27.

The nose and main gear units.

Rear view of the S-37, showing to advantage the stabilators at maximum downward deflection. The closely spaced engines are noteworthy.

Mikoyan MFI and Sukhoi S-37

At the MAKS-97 airshow NPO Vympel demonstrated the K-74 short-range AAM based on the familiar R-73 (AA-11 *Archer*). The new missile differs in having a new IR seeker head with a 120° field of view (instead of 80° or 90° on the earlier model). The seeker is also more sensitive, increasing target acquisition range by 30% (to 40 km/21.6 nm). Development began in the mid-1980s; the first launches of the K-74 took place in 1994, and preparations for production were underway as of this writing. Additionally, NPO Vympel is working on a range of 'dogfight AAMs' featuring TVC which will give them extreme agility.

Like the other multi-role tactical aircraft developed by Sukhoi (the Su-30MK, Su-35 and Su-37), the future combat version of the S-37 is designed to carry air-to-surface weapons as well. These include precision weapons (TV- or laser-guided air-to-surface missiles and guided bombs), anti-shipping missiles (such as the 3M80 Moskit) and anti-radiation missiles (such as the Kh-15). The wings will incorporate hardpoints for such ordnance or drop tanks.

S-37 Specifications

Length, inc air data boom	22.6 m (74 ft 2 in)
Wing span	16.7 m (54 ft 9½ in)
Height on ground	6.4 m (21 ft 0 in)
Wing area, m² (ft²)	56.00 (602.15)
Normal TOW, kg (lb)	24,000-25,670 (52,910-56,591)
MTOW, kg (lb)	34,000 (74,955)
Top speed, km/h (kts):	
at S/L	1,400 (756.75)
at high altitude	Mach 1.6
Service ceiling, m (ft)	18,000 (59,055)
Effective range, km (nm)	3,300 (1,783)
G limit	+9.0

Like its 'competitor', the MFI, the S-37 is to carry most of the weapons internally. The weapons bay doors are clearly visible in the photo above.

Note: These figures are provisional and are based on figures reported in the popular press

S-37: Proud Bird of Prey

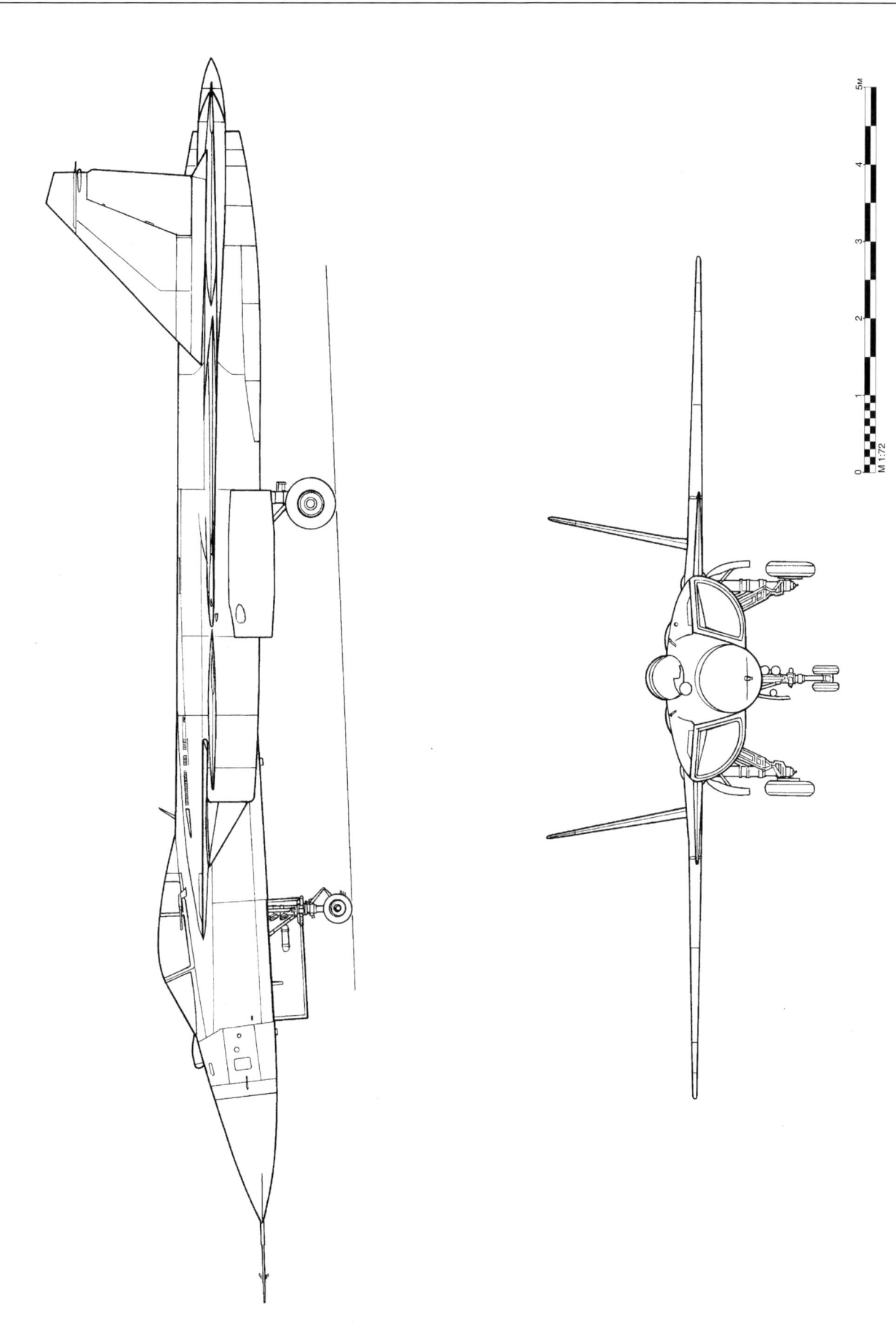

Port and front views of the S-37 Berkoot development aircraft.

Mikoyan MFI and Sukhoi S-37

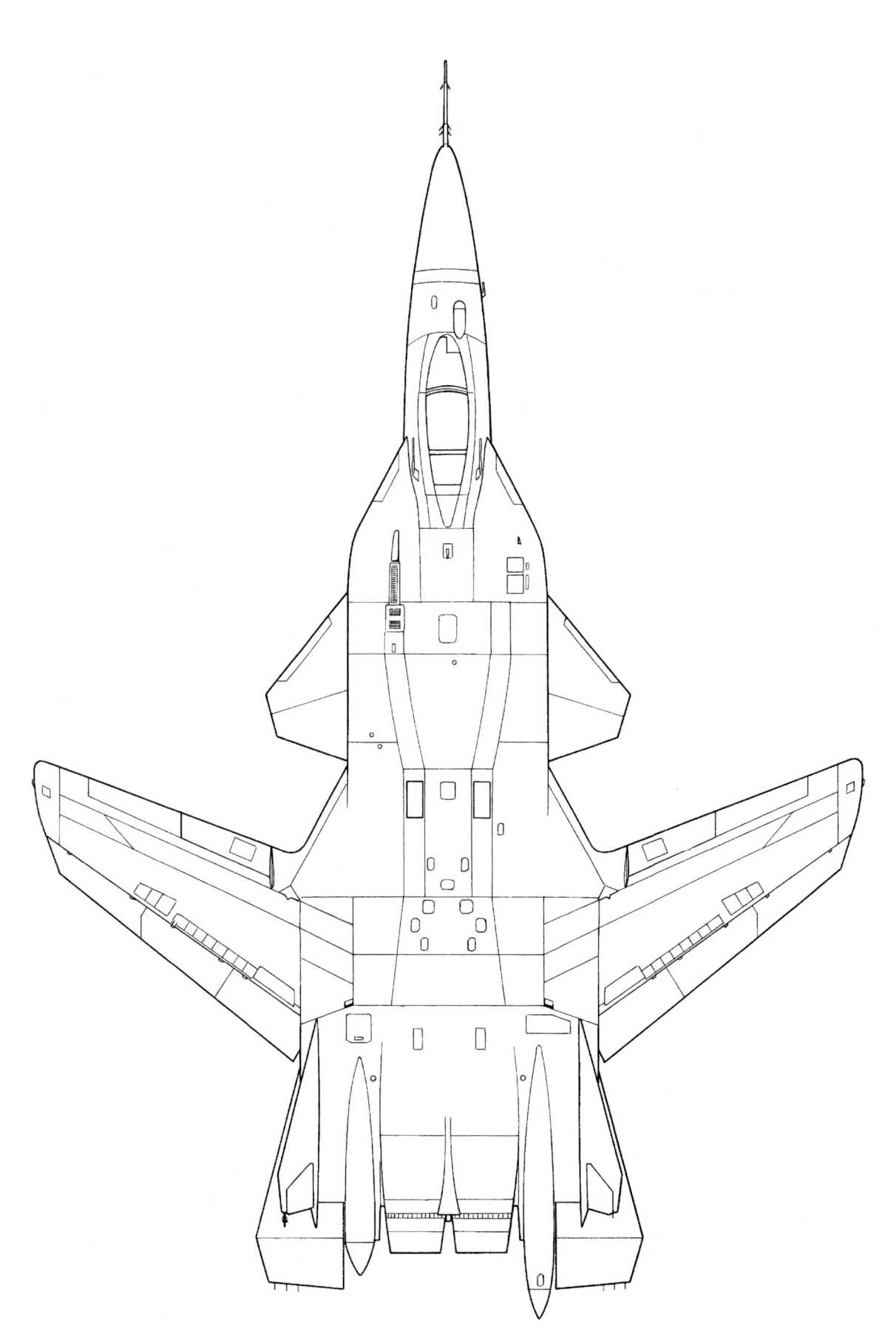

Top view of the S-37 Berkoot.

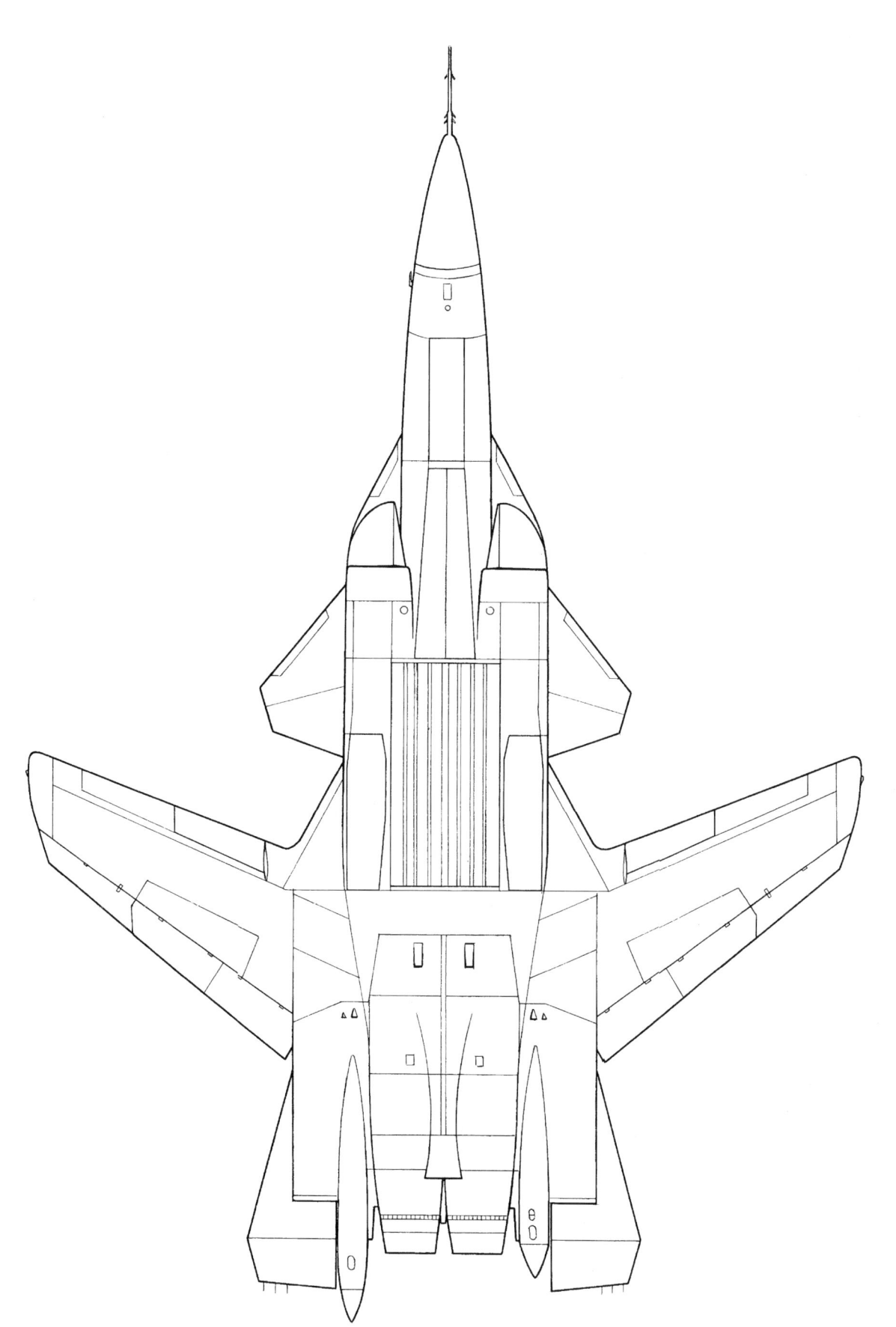

S-37: Proud Bird of Prey

Bottom view of the S-37 Berkoot.

Mikoyan MFI and Sukhoi S-37

Above and below: The S-37's flat black colour scheme did not allow observers to see the internal weapons bay when lighting conditions were poor.

'To be or not to be?..'

Mikoyan MFI and Sukhoi S-37

Even though it is purely an experimental aircraft, the Berkoot is without doubt a major step in Russian aviation development.

The step-by-step strategy of fifth-generation fighter development chosen by the Mikoyan and Sukhoi design bureaux is best suited to the current economic situation in Russia. In fact, it is the only possible strategy; neither company would manage to create a fully capable fifth-generation fighter as a 'clean sheet of paper' project. Trying its hand on a technology demonstrator highlights critical design aspects, enabling the company to concentrate on them. Proven technologies and design features used on state-of-the-art fighters may be employed in less critical areas, cutting development costs and saving time.

On 17th September 1998 NPO Lyul'ka-Saturn and the Rybinsk Motors Joint-Stock Company signed an agreement at the latter company's seat in Rybinsk (Yaroslavl' Region). (This company combines the Rybinsk aero engine design bureau (RKBM – **Ryb**inskoye kon**strook**torskoye byu**ro** mo**tor**ostroyeniya) and the Rybinsk engine factory producing, for example the Solov'yov D-30KU turbofan powering the Il'yushin IL-62M Classic and Tupolev Tu-154M Careless airliners and the D-30KP powering the IL-76 Candid transport and its derivatives.) The agreement, which concerned production of the AL-41F engine, was a major milestone for the Russian defence industry in more ways than one. Given Russia's (and hence the national aerospace industry's) protracted financial crisis, the decision to launch production of the first indigenous fifth-generation fighter engine was a sensation in itself. In effect, the choice of the AL-41F as the 'baseline' engine has set the general trend for future advanced combat aircraft design in Russia. This engine, which is due to enter production in 2003-04, clears the way for the LFS (**lyoh**kiy fronto**voy** samo**lyot** – light tactical aircraft) programme under which RSK MiG and the Sukhoi OKB are currently developing the Russian Air Force's main light combat aircraft of the future. What is more, Sukhoi reportedly plan to re-engine the Su-34 (Su-32FN) multi-role strike aircraft with AL-41Fs; the seven examples built to date in Novosibirsk are powered by AL-31Fs, like most other members of the Su-27 family.

The decision to launch production of the AL-41F in spite of the Russian MoD's and defence industry's problems indicates that the Ministry of Defence has worked out a more or less realistic upgrade and re-equipment plan for the VVS. The plan capitalises on new engines and advanced avionics. This approach not only facilitates development of new-generation combat aircraft but also allows the capabilities of existing ones to be expanded rapidly and cheaply.

AVPK Sukhoi and Sukhoi OKB General Director Mikhail A. Pogosyan calls his brainchild (remember, he was S-37 project chief most of the time) a 'research aircraft'. In his opinion, the S-37's test results will help Sukhoi engineers to define the next-generation fighter's layout. RSK MiG General Designer Nikolay F. Nikitin voiced similar ideas, saying that 'many of the features incorporated in the [izdeliye] 1.44 experimental fighter may find use on the future fifth-generation fighter'.

So, what future lies ahead for Russian military aviation in the 21st century? Even now it is obvious that neither the Mikoyan MFI (1.42), nor the Sukhoi S-37 can suit the

'To be or not to be?..'

Russian Air Force's needs. Their development and test cycle has dragged on too long. In the meantime, both the Air Force's operational requirements and the Russian fifth-generation fighter concept have changed somewhat, making these aircraft obsolete before they even had a chance. In an interview to Nezavisimoye voyennoye obozreniye, GosNII AS General Director Yevgeniy Fedosov gave the following derisive comment on the three main criteria of fifth-generation fighter design used earlier (ultra-manoeuvrability, supercruise capability and stealth):

'I assert that this is stuff and nonsense. These three criteria are irrelevant; they were formulated by people with an airframer's mentality who cannot see beyond progress in that area of aircraft design. The Su-30 with vectoring nozzles has already achieved ultra-manoeuvrability; it is a kind of standard-setter in that respect. Forward-swept wings or anything else, for that matter, will not improve agility significantly [beyond the Su-30]. Besides, ultra-manoeuvrability does not give any particular benefits in a dogfight – apart from a slightly expanded envelope within which close-range weapons may be used, perhaps. But then there is a heavy price to pay for this, because you have to ensure smooth engine operation in extremely demanding flight conditions. It takes a lot to create such an engine. I'm not suggesting that we should give up what we already have, but there's no real point in going further in this direction.'

As for supercruise capability, Fedosov says, 'Really this flight mode is needed primarily for patrolling large spaces on air defence missions (which, incidentally, admittedly applies to Russia). High speed is required to quickly intercept intruders at long range. However, in the case of an aircraft grossing up to 20 tons [44,091 lb] there is probably no need to strive for supercruise capability by all means.'

Being, as it is, one of Russia's top experts on avionics suites and systems, Academician Fedosov strongly believes that in the current circumstances the aircraft companies should concentrate on developing a versatile combat aircraft with a normal TOW of 20 tons at the most. He cites several reasons for this. Economics are the main reason; there is no point in creating a new fighter solely for the home market. Heavy fighters like the Su-27 and MiG-31 will remain in service with the Russian air arm for many years yet. Outside Russia, however, aircraft in this 'weight category' are of interest only to nations with a huge territory and a considerable military potential, such as India and mainland China. The other CIS republics have no use for such aircraft. The bottom line is that in order to keep unit costs down Russia will need to build relatively large numbers of the fifth-generation fighter and target the export market as well – which is already crowded. This means the fighter will need to be a competitive answer to the USA's future Joint Strike Fighter (JSF).

The latest American fighters illustrate this point. The F-22A Raptor, which is entering low-rate initial production (LRIP) as of this writing, is a heavy fighter designed to operate over large territories, away from its base (ie, in areas with few airfields). It is unlikely to attract export orders because, at about US$ 200 million per copy, it is outra-

AVPK Sukhoi General Director and SUkhoi OKB chief Mikhail Pogosyan says the S-37's test programme will help the engineers to define the outlook of the next-generation fighter.

Mikoyan MFI and Sukhoi S-37

This page and opposite: The Berkoot taxies in after a demo flight at the MAKS-99 airshow. These views show how the canards and stabilators move in concert. Note that both fin leading edges are black now.

'To be or not to be?..'

Mikoyan MFI and Sukhoi S-37

This page: The S-37 Berkoot makes its first public appearance at Moscow-Tushino on Aviation Day (15th August 1999).

'To be or not to be?..'

This page: Another test flight has been successfully completed.

Mikoyan MFI and Sukhoi S-37

Development of Russia's fighter technology demonstrators has taken far longer than anticipated. Yet it was not in vain, as these aircraft have helped Russian companies to outline the priority areas of fifth-generation fighter design.

geously expensive; there is hardly a nation (besides the USA) which can afford it. The Raptor has supercruise capability, whereas the JSF will probably lack it.

Russian experts believe the JSF is targeted primarily at the markets traditionally served by Russian and European 'fighter makers' (not at the NATO's air arms) and is thus intended to terminally drive the Russian and European competitors into the ground. To this end the aircraft is aggressively priced at US$ 30-38 million, depending on the version; the broad objective is to offer potential customers a fifth-generation fighter at the price of a fourth-generation fighter. Incidentally, this view is shared by some European experts who have been voicing the 'beware the JSF' opinion ever since the programme was launched.

Regarding the stealth issue, Russian analysts and experts (primarily Ministry of Defence experts) disagree with their US colleagues. Gulf War experience and Operation Allied Force (the bombing of Serbia and Kosovo in March-May 1999) show that in a modern war the first wave of attacking aircraft launches air-to-ground missiles when still beyond the range of enemy air defences. If the enemy's AD system is destroyed or substantially damaged by this first attack, any aircraft – stealthy or not – can get through. Hence both Russia and the USA require their AD systems to be capable of detecting and destroying targets with an RCS less than 0.1 m² (1.07 ft²).

What is more, the Lockheed F-117A Nighthawk shows that stealth has too high a price, as 'stealthy' design features compromise other crucial aspects – speed, weapons load, agility and handling. An aircraft's RCS is affected considerably by various electronic systems (ECM, electronic intelligence (ELINT), navigation and communications) and their aerials which may reveal the aircraft's position. The smallest RCS attained to date for a manned aircraft is approximately 0.3 m² (3.22 ft²). Hence the latest military doctrines envisage the use of unmanned combat aerial vehicles (UCAVs) tasked with suppression of enemy air defences (SEAD) which act as 'outriders', clearing the way for manned aircraft.

The opinions of Russian combat aircraft designers on the concepts used by the two JSF contenders (the Boeing X-32 and the Lockheed Martin X-35, both of which entered flight test in the autumn of 2000) vary. To reduce RCS both aircraft feature internal weapons bays, which places a limit on the weapons load; however, using external hardpoints to carry more bombs and missiles would ruin stealth. Besides, designing the airframe to minimise RCS inevitably affects its aerodynamics, which in turn has a negative effect on the aircraft's manoeuvrability.

So, where should the priorities lie? In other words, what qualities should be sacrificed to gain what?

Academician Yevgeniy Fedosov says the avionics suite will be the fifth-generation fighter's most important component. (Of course, one has to remember that he is, putting it mildly, not exactly impartial, being chief of Russia's top R&D establishment in avionics.) Fedosov highly rates American expertise in this field, especially the fact that '...they have switched to controlling the aircraft's mission equipment in cyberspace as a matter of principle'. This, in his opinion, is the rationale for a fifth-generation combat aircraft. Active phased-array radars, high-powered processors, computer systems installed on airborne command posts and airborne warning and control system (AWACS) aircraft, CDs with databases on all possible flight profiles, terrain and tactical situation display systems – all of this combines to create the abovementioned cyberspace for the pilot. The fighter's multi-mode displays have to show not only the aircraft's position with respect to the terrain but also targets and threats for complete situational awareness.

Integration with command, control, communications and intelligence (C³I) systems is a key requirement for the fifth-generation fighter's avionics suite. Tactical information will be downloaded to the pilot by data link from AWACS and reconnaissance aircraft. Thus reconnaissance aircraft and strike aircraft are integrated into a single reconnaissance/strike system which, says Fedosov, will be 'the main qualitative improvement of the fifth-generation fighter'.

Unfortunately, Russia effectively lacks the electronic components required to create this type of avionics. The Russian electronics

Above: **The Lockheed Martin X-35A JSF contender during a test flight.**

Below: **The Boeing JSF (the X-32A) at the rollout ceremony, showing the starboard weapons bay.**

Mikoyan MFI and Sukhoi S-37

AVPK Sukhoi General Director Mikhail Pogosyan says the company is now 'testing and verifying advanced technologies on the S-37 Berkoot FSW aircraft; these will be incorporated into Russia's next-generation fighter'.

industry is no better off than the aerospace industry, suffering from the tell-tale crisis just like everybody else – not to mention the fact that the Soviet Union was 'traditionally' behind the West in this area. (Soviet avionics weigh about half as much again as their Western counterparts, hence the old joke about Soviet microchips being the largest microchips in the world.)

Nevertheless, several Russian avionics companies have made good progress lately. By the year 2000 the national electronics industry was to create on-board digital computer systems which are sufficiently compact and lightweight to suit the airframers' demands, fast (processing dozens of billions of commands per second) – and, importantly, use only locally-made components. As for the latest models of Russian radars, they are more than a match for – and, in some respects, better than – state-of-the-art Western radars.

Meanwhile, by 2002 the USA plan to launch production of an active phased-array radar. This will, in effect, be the core of an ECM-resistant 360° surveillance system for the American fifth-generation fighter. The aircraft's radar system will utilise the integrated aperture principle, ie, all antennas and high-frequency pulse generators are integrated into a common system to minimise the number of HF emitters. This reduces revealing electromagnetic pulse (EMP) emissions, reducing the aircraft's RCS and aiding stealth, and makes the system more versatile. Strike aircraft equipped with integrated aperture systems will operate in groups; one aircraft in the group will act as a 'mini-AWACS', enabling the others to maintain radio silence.

The possibility of creating integrated aperture systems in Russia is open to doubt, and not only for technological reasons. Such systems can only work when the number of wavebands used is kept to a minimum, significantly reducing the number of antennas/aerials. Russia, however, uses the byzantine system inherited from the Soviet Union – long ago the Soviet Armed Forces General Headquarters allocated separate wavebands to each service 'to stop them from getting in each other's way'. (Alas, the road to hell is paved with good intentions...) Besides, development of integrated aperture systems will require huge investments, which is impracticable in Russian conditions – unless the defence industry is restructured and various enterprises participating in the fifth-generation fighter programme work as one team (to use Boeing's JSF advertising slogan).

As already mentioned, the Russian 'fighter makers' – Sukhoi, Mikoyan and Yakovlev (yes, Yakovlev are still in the game!) – are now concentrating on the LFS light tactical aircraft, a sort of 'anti-JSF'; this will evidently be Russia's fifth-generation fighter. Once again, each company is working on several PD project versions. After the Russian Air Force has reviewed them, the winner of the contest may be announced in the near future. As RSK MiG chief Nikolay Nikitin said, no matter who wins the LFS tender, the aircraft will most likely be produced by several companies (including former competitors) as a joint effort. This will be the cheapest and quickest way to get the fighter into the air, into production and into service. Mikhail Pogosyan probably has similar views.

Apparently Russian aerospace companies (and their US counterparts, for that matter) will inevitably have to join forces when it comes to building the fifth-generation fighter. Still, even if such a co-operation programme is developed, the big question remains how Russia will manage to raise funding – and how much money will be needed. Russian airframers quote a figure of several hundred million dollars; the avionics designers are more pessimistic, stating that at least US$ 2 billion will be required because of the high complexity of the latest data processing and presentation systems.

How can Russia finance the LFS programme, given the rather meagre defence budget? The solution seems to be arms exports, primarily sales of combat aircraft. Also, Russia may have to seek risk-sharing partners abroad which will shoulder part of the costs. Such nations as China and India, which have a history of building Soviet/Russian aircraft under licence (including Generation 4+ fighters for which they have recently acquired manufacturing rights), may wish to participate in the development of the Russian fifth-generation fighter. Technological co-operation with some West European nations which may find it difficult to create a similar fighter on their own is also possible. As Yevgeniy Fedosov put it, 'we need to borrow technologies from the West, money from the East and make it an international programme in which anyone can participate'.

Despite the shift in priorities towards the LFS, tests of the Mikoyan and Sukhoi heavy fighter technology demonstrators will go on as planned. In fact, Sukhoi have even managed to get the S-37 included into the Russian MoD's orderbook for 1999; this gives it 'official' status (as the reader remembers, the aircraft had been developed as a private venture until now) and should make more funding available for the test programme. RSK MiG are not so lucky. Indeed, rumours have started circulating that getting the 1.44 off the ground was purely a matter of prestige for the company, that the aircraft cannot be brought up to scratch and will be donated to the Russian Air Force Museum in Monino near Moscow after a few more flights.

Still, the Mikoyan 1.44 and the Sukhoi S-37 Berkoot will not be developed further; the know-how accumulated with these types will be used only for developing subsequent projects. Thus the two aircraft are not really fifth-generation fighter prototypes but rather testbeds for a wide spectrum of new technologies to be used on Russian aircraft of the 21st century – civil as well as military.

Mikoyan MFI and Sukhoi S-37

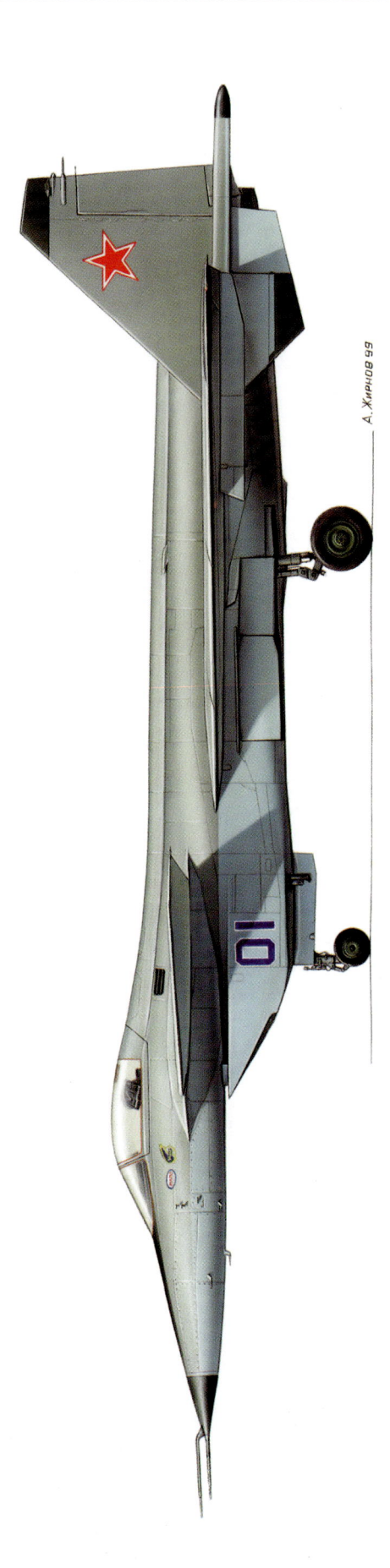

Port and front views of the *izdeliye* 1.44 experimental aircraft.

'To be or not to be?..'

Top view of the izdeliye 1.44 experimental aircraft.

Mikoyan MFI and Sukhoi S-37

Port and front views of the S-37 Berkoot development aircraft.

'To be or not to be?..'

Top view of the S-37 Berkoot.

We hope you enjoyed this book ...

Midland Publishing titles are edited and designed by an experienced and enthusiastic team of specialists.

Further titles are in preparation but we always welcome ideas from authors or readers for books they would like to see published.

In addition, our associate, Midland Counties Publications, offers an exceptionally wide range of aviation, spaceflight, astronomy, military, naval and transport books and videos for sale by mail-order around the world.

For a copy of the appropriate catalogue, or to order further copies of this book, and any of many other Midland Publishing titles, please write, telephone, fax or e-mail to:

Midland Counties Publications
4 Watling Drive, Hinckley,
Leics, LE10 3EY, England

Tel: (+44) 01455 254 450
Fax: (+44) 01455 233 737
E-mail: midlandbooks@compuserve.com
www.midlandcountiessuperstore.com

US distribution by Specialty Press – see page 2.

ILYUSHIN IL-76
Russia's Versatile Airlifter

Yefim Gordon & Dmitriy Komissarov

The Soviet Union's answer to the Lockheed Starlifter first flew in 1971 and has become familiar both in its intended military guise and as a commercial freighter. It has also been developed as the IL-78 for aerial refuelling, and in AEW and other versions.

There is not only a full development history and technical description, but extensive tables detailing each aircraft built, with c/n, serial and so on, and detailed notes on every operator, both civil and military, and their fleets.

Softback, 280 x 215 mm, 160 pages
c250 b/w and colour photos, drawings
1 85780 106 7   **£19.95/US $34.95**

Aerofax
MIKOYAN-GUREVICH MiG-15

Yefim Gordon

In this Aerofax, compiled from a wealth of first-hand Russian sources, there is a comprehensive history of every evolution of the Soviet Union's swept-wing fighter and its service. Notably in this volume, there are tables listing intricate details of many individual aircraft, a concept which would have been unthinkable in any publications only a few years ago.

There is extensive and detailed photo coverage, again from Russian sources, almost all of which is previously unseen.

Softback, 280 x 215 mm, 160 pages
211 b/w, 18 colour photos, 7pp colour sideviews, 18pp b/w drawings
1 85780 105 9   **£17.95/US $29.95**

FLANKERS
The New Generation

Yefim Gordon

The multi-role Su-30 and Su-35 and thrust-vectoring Su-37 are described in detail, along with the 'big head' Su-23FN/Su-34 tactical bomber, the Su-27K (Su-33) shipborne fighter and its two-seat combat trainer derivative, the Su-27KUB. The book also describes the customised versions developed for foreign customers – the Su-30KI (Su-27KI), the Su-30MKI for India, the Su-30MKK for China and the latest Su-35UB.

Softback, 280 x 215 mm, 128 pages
250 colour, 6 b/w photographs, drawings/side-views
1 85780 121 0   **£18.95/US $27.95**

SOVIET COMBAT AIRCRAFT OF THE SECOND WORLD WAR
Volume One: Single-Engined Fighters

Yefim Gordon and Dmitri Khazanov

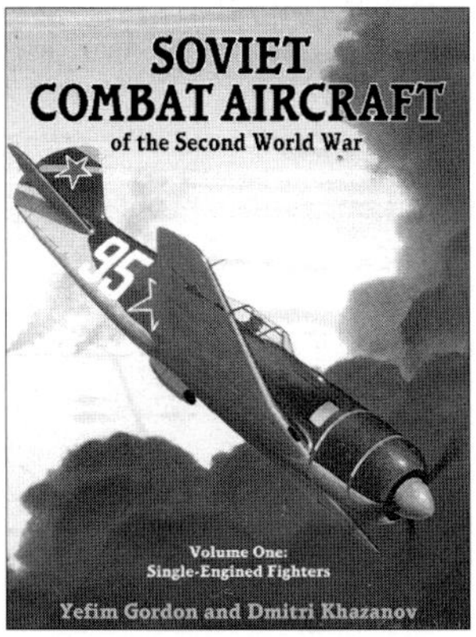

Arranged by manufacturer, this includes the prototype and operational products of famous designers such as Lavochkin, Mikoyan and Yakovlev as well as the lesser known, such as the Bereznyak-Isaev rocket propelled fighter.

Rich Russian sources including manufacturers, flight test establishments and Soviet air force and naval aviation records provide a wealth of new material, much of which rewrites previously held Western views.

Hardback, 282 x 213 mm, 184 pages
358 b/w photos; 28 layout diagrams,
16 full colour side views
1 85780 083 4   **£24.95/US $39.95**

SOVIET COMBAT AIRCRAFT OF THE SECOND WORLD WAR
Twin Eng Fighters, Attack Acft & Bombers

Yefim Gordon and Dmitri Khazanov

Arranged by designer, this includes the products of famous names such as Ilyushin, Petlyakov and Tupolev as well as lesser known types.

In his introduction, Bill Gunston explains the unique nature of Soviet aviation, the politics and strategies and the problems created by the vastness of the country – and confirms that the two volumes of *Soviet Combat Aircraft* are set to become the premier reference on this facet of aviation history.

Hardback, 282 x 213 mm, 176 pages
285 b/w photos; 27 layout diagrams;
17 full colour side views
1 85780 084 2   **£24.95/US $39.95**

THE X-PLANES X-1 to X-45
New, totally revised third edition

Jay Miller

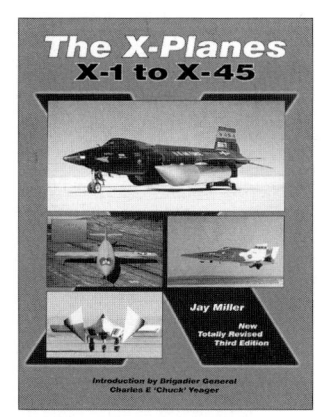

This new, totally revised and updated version of 'The X-Planes' contains a detailed and authoritative account of every single X-designated aircraft. There is considerable new, and newly-declassified information on all X-Planes.

Each aircraft is described fully with coverage of history, specifications, propulsion systems and disposition. Included are rare cockpit illustrations. Each X-Plane is also illustrated by a detailed multi-view drawing.

Hardback, 280 x 216mm, 440 pages
c850 b/w, 52 colour photographs,
approximately 110 drawings
1 85780 109 1   **£39.95/US $59.95**

SOVIET X-PLANES

Yefim Gordon & Bill Gunston

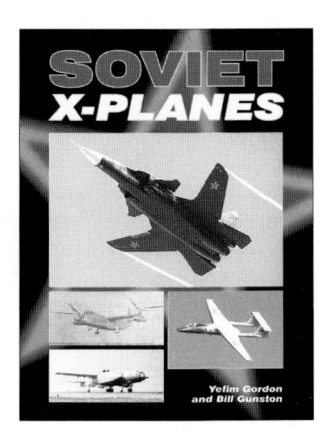

A detailed review of Soviet experimental aircraft from the early 1900s through to the latest Russian prototypes of today.

The book is the first to collect the stories of the more important Soviet experimental aircraft into one volume. Working from original sources the authors have produced an outstanding reference which although concentrating on hardware also includes many unflown projects. About 150 types are described, each with relevant data, and including many three-view drawings.

Hardback, 282 x 213mm, 240 pages
355 b/w, 50 colour photos; 200 dwgs
1 85780 099 0   **£29.95/US $44.95**